TAILS FROM THE HEART

TAILS FROM THE HEART

Stories, poems, and artwork

An anthology presented by Peninsula Friends Of Animals

iUniverse, Inc.

New York Bloomington Shanghai

Tails from the Heart

Stories, poems, and artwork

Copyright © 2008 by Peninsula Friends of Animals

iUniverse books may be ordered through booksellers or by contacting:

iUniverse
1663 Liberty Drive
Bloomington, IN 47403
www.iuniverse.com
1-800-Authors (1-800-288-4677)

COVER ART: "Maggie and Hope" by Linda Kemp

ISBN: 978-0-595-51810-4 (pbk)
ISBN: 978-0-595-62042-5 (ebk)

Printed in the United States of America

A special thank you to Nancy Campbell for suggesting the title of this book and for her tireless work with homeless animals.

And to Susan Skaggs for her year of dedication, typing, editing and prodding everyone involved to get this book off the ground.

Thanks also to our panel of judges: Erika Hamerquist, Morgan Van Dyke, Joan Worley and Susan Skaggs, for their editorial comments, good humor and assistance, as well as our "4 Paws Award" judge, Elizabeth Ann Scarborough.

CONTENTS

Introduction...xi

Haiku for the Fallen.. 1
    by Ann Gilson

Miss Behavin'.. 2
    Dee Smiley

Peter's Escape Escapade Turns Eerily Risky................................. 3
    by Bonnie L. Erickson

Angel Above My Head.. 7
    by James V. Randazzo

Princess Ashley.. 9
    Phyllis Blakely

Something Good To Be.. 10
    by Cullyn Foxlee

Kittens... 11
    by Tina Oaks

Ruckus.. 13
    by Karen Grimsley

His Day... 15
    by Kevin Torres

Please Come Back.. 19
    Dee Smiley

Rescue Me... 20
    by Joe Wright

Call Me Anthropomorphic 21
    by Deborah Daline

Max and Bandit 24
    by Beverlee Benbow

Dogs of My Childhood 27
    by Barbara Pelett

Summer "Inspurration" 30
    by Mary Margolis

Buttons 31
    Raven O'Keefe

The Things That Don't Really Matter 32
    by Diane Lopez

Precarious Beginnings 35
    by Ann Chang

Ian & Moss 37
    Raven O'Keefe

My Shelter Dog 38
    by Terry Metheny

Matt's Cat 43
    by Vern Ward

Blue Cat 43
    Ali Seeber-Lestage

The Irish Cat 44
    by Ann Gilson

Dram, A Rescue 49
    by Lynn Calhoun

Butch, the Canine Parish Assistant 54
    by Ruth Gordon

John & Shadow 58
    Raven O'Keefe

My Mother's Freckles.. 59

    by DeeAnn Nelson

Suzie 60

    by Terry Kush

Metaphor Mouse.. 62

    by Michael Marcus

Billy 71

    by Elizabeth Fletcher Barlow

Dad and Billy.. 72

    Submitted by Elizabeth Fletcher Barlow

Midnight Snow in Time 73

    by Ann Gilson

Brighty.. 79

    by Cynthia Bend

Brighty.. 81

    Torry Bend

Requiem from Bud for His Master.. 82

    by Shirley Jean Coker

The Great Chicken Rescue... 83

    by Craig William Andrews

Murphy Brown ... and Black and White 85

    by Kim McBride

Make My Day... 94

    Raven O'Keefe

Dogs 95

    by Linda Wentz

Cats A-plenty 97

    by Sally M. Harris

Day Dreaming Georgie 98

    Nancy O'Gorman

Searching 99
    by Ann Gilson

MEET THE JUDGES

Finders Keepers.. 125
    By Erika Hamerquist

Greyling.. 153
    Raven O'Keefe

Anatomy Lesson at Young's Dairy 154
    by Morgan Van Dyke

Moss & Minnie 156
    Raven O'Keefe

Divine Feline 157
    by Susan M. Skaggs

Siamese 168
    Raven O'Keefe

Ambrose 169
    by Joan Worley

Bubby 185
    Raven O'Keefe

Mu Mao and the Court Oracle 186
    by Elizabeth Ann Scarborough

The Artists 199

Introduction

Peninsula Friends of Animals was established in December 1999 and became a 501 (c) (3) nonprofit in 2001. PFOA is a no-kill rescue group made up of dedicated volunteers who recognize the need to curb pet overpopulation on Washington state's North Olympic Peninsula.

Since then, PFOA has expanded to include Safe Haven (opened in February 2004), a temporary home to cats and kittens in need of adoption. PFOA also has a trap/neuter/release program for feral cats, low cost or free spaying and neutering, emergency medical care for pets of low-income residents, and emergency pet food assistance to owners of companion animals.

PFOA receives no tax money and depends entirely on the generous help of those who support our mission.

You can be part of the solution. In America 3 to 4 million cats and dogs are put to death each year simply because there aren't enough homes for them. All profit from the sale of this book goes toward housing cats at Safe Haven as they await adoption and to PFOA's spay/neuter programs.

To Give:

Peninsula Friends of Animals
P. O. Box 404
Sequim, WA 98382
www.safehavenPFOA.org
360-452-0414 (message phone)

About our book: Stories, poems and artwork in *Tails from the Heart* are contest winners selected by a panel of volunteer judges. Written material was then edited and sent to Nebula-Award-winning author Elizabeth Ann Scarborough. She selected the "Best of the Best" to receive "4 Paws Awards." Stories by Ms. Scarborough and the contest judges can be found in the "Meet the Judges" section at the end of the book.

4 PAWS AWARD
Best in Show
First Place, Poetry

HAIKU FOR THE FALLEN

by Ann Gilson

My son will not come

Home again.

Never again.

His little dog cries.

Ann Gilson is a retired university librarian who has been active in animal rescue for more than sixty years. Her twin passions are books and cats, and she cares for a large collection of each.

MISS BEHAVIN'

Dee Smiley

PETER'S ESCAPE ESCAPADE TURNS EERILY RISKY

by Bonnie L. Erickson

Peter flew. Brushing my nose with his wings, he soared out the door of the "silver bullet," bidding me farewell as he gained altitude, and slaloming the evergreens lining our driveway. Freedom. Finally after all those years!

The dishes I was carrying crashed to the ground as I lunged for him. I heard thunder in the distance, and my heart stopped. No way could Peter survive on his own. Not with rain and cold coming.

Eleven years earlier, Peter, a Quaker or Monk parrot, was hatched and hand-fed in central Florida, the land of lightning and storms. He came to live with us on our ranch near Brooksville at the tender age of six months, and reaped all the benefits of Bird of the House: big cage with an "open door" policy. His favorite delicacies: pizza and spaghetti. His staples: fruit, veggies, and vitamin coated seeds.

Peter had dead-on aim which allowed him to "bomb" the dog with food or poop from a vantage point on the cage perch. He talked in sentences, vocally begging for his share while we humans ate, and at bedtime demanding to be covered and the TV extinguished for the night.

At eleven, Peter's life and ours changed. My husband, Red, and I retired, sold our ranch, and decided to return to Washington. The Olympic Peninsula this time. Time to build a home on our little five-acre parcel in the foothills.

Since our cross-country trek would include Peter plus our Yorkie, Sparkle, and kitty, Grey Kitty, a travel trailer was needed. We chose the Airstream—our silver bullet—with two thoughts in mind: we'd live in it for a few months while the house was being built, and there was a perfect shelf for Peter's new traveling cage.

Across the United States in July, 2003. Hot! Sparkle, Grey Kitty, and Peter, secure in crates seatbelted in the truck's back seat, lavished in air-conditioning. Peter usually snoozed, his crate covered with a thin sheet to repel direct air, but when jarred awake by rough roads, he'd squawk in outrage. "What are you doin'?" "Hello!" "Peeter. Peeter. Peeter."

Every night we settled in a new RV park, and Peter, in his traveling cage, perched in his perfect spot on the galley shelf.

We all arrived safely at our destination, but delays slowed the home-building project to a crawl. By late October we were still living in the Airstream. There was still plenty of daylight and warmth, though, so Red and I occupied ourselves with building fence lines and parking-out the lower three acres.

One Saturday we decided to take a lunch break outside at our picnic table. Could that really be thunder in the distance? Oh, but it was so sunny and warm, we couldn't resist taking advantage of the Indian summer weather.

There was one hard and fast rule concerning living in the trailer with Peter and the others: Peter could only be out of his cage while *both* Red and I were inside. Also the screen door must be locked. Peter still had his flight feathers for safety in case he needed to flee the "others." But today Peter had protested so loudly at being caged while everyone else was enjoying outside, I had broken my own rule and opened Peter's door so he could sit quietly in his cage taking it all in.

Our picnic lunch finished, I proceeded to clear the table. With both arms balancing dishes, I opened the screen door with my pinkie finger. Whoosh! A green blur. Peter had seen his opportunity, and he'd flown. Dishes crashing, I screamed for Red. I ran as fast as I could in my flip-flops on the gravel, yelling. But Peter had already disappeared.

Four hours I trudged up and down our road and driveway. "Peter, Peter, Pretty Pete, what are you doin', pretty bird?" non-stop I called. No answer. Dusk descended. Thunder rumbled and now there was lightning as well. The irony of it all! Surely we had left all that back in Florida! Now Peter was lost in a "foreign" environment as darkness approached, the temperature dropped, and rain fell. It hadn't done any of this since we had arrived in July! Why now?

I quizzed a fellow down the road if per chance he'd seen a small green parrot. As we both studied the sky, he said, "Sorry, no. But that's an odd silhouette flying over there."

Totally dejected, I made my final trudge up our driveway. One last hoarse, "Peter, Peter, Pretty Bird."

Fifty feet from the trailer I heard the answer. "Peeter." Again, "Peeter." I hear well. Red sees well, so he was the first to spot him. There he was! Forty feet up in a cedar tree, Peter was perched on a branch, hugging the tree trunk. Evidently he'd flown a circular route for several miles then returned. Our joy at finding him faded as we recognized the real challenge was still before us.

No way was Peter going to leave that tree. We hoisted his cage containing seeds and water. Nothing. We scattered seeds on the picnic table. No go. We coaxed. Nope. The night grew darker, chillier, and a constant rain fell. If we cut the tree we might kill him. If he lived through the night—we had owls, too—he'd likely succumb to exposure.

I doubt any of us slept that night. I cried. Red was pensive. Peter hugged his tree. We checked on him every two hours with a flashlight. Before daylight at 5:00 a.m. I announced that we would succeed. "I'll call a tree service," I said.

Hoping not to find a pile of green feathers beneath the tree, I checked on Peter one last time. He was still there. It was now 5:30 a.m. on a Sunday morning. I rummaged through the Yellow Pages searching for tree services. I found a bunch. By 6:00 a.m. I was dialing. One by one I went through the list. The odds were against us, considering the day, considering the time. A number of message machines answered. One fellow laughed and said, "Good luck," then hung up. Another reminded me it was Sunday. The list grew shorter. Then fortune struck! A lady answered my call. I explained the situation. She paused, then, obviously sensing my desperation, told me she was certain her son would help us out, but he was at the hospital. His wife was giving birth. She said she'd call him; she was sure he could figure out a solution. I waited. No call back. I waited longer. Still no call back.

When I could contain myself no longer, I called the woman back, and she asked why I hadn't been answering my phone. I said that it hadn't rung. She said that both she and her son had tried to call twice—no answer. She had the correct number. Land line. Always worked before. I could obviously call out. I had paid the phone bill! Could anything *else* possibly go wrong?

She would call her son again and get his solution, she promised. I would wait ten minutes, then call her back. This worked. An experienced climber would be sent from the Joyce area to attempt the rescue.

When the truck arrived, a young fellow bounded out, gathering equipment as he asked for details. He said he'd rescued kittens and an Iguana, but a parrot was a first. We took him to Peter's cedar tree. Its trunk was only six inches in diameter, so he climbed a nearby tree, and secured the trees together ready to rappel. Peter watched these preparations intently. When the fellow was in position, arms outstretched just inches away ... Peter flew. But now at least there were three sets of eyes following him, and we all saw where he landed: another tree, an alder this time. Another climb, another flight. Thankfully, Peter was landing lower in the trees. Next rescue attempt: a trout net lashed to a long thin alder sapling. Just about had him. But Peter flew. As we all talked about him, Peter flew yet again. Only he was obviously tiring from his ordeal, and this time he fluttered to the ground. Red walked over to him, scooped him up and headed for the trailer. Back inside his cage one tired, hungry Peter ate and drank with fervor. Then he fluffed up, tucked his head under his wing and snoozed.

I cheerfully paid the climber for his labors, and he departed. Red and I crashed. Peter? Nothing wrong with him. He woke us both a bit later with: "What are you doin'? Peeter. Peeter."

Bonnie L. Erickson is a former chemical analyst and marine sales agent. She lives near Port Angeles, Washington, with her husband, dog, cat, donkey and "Peter" parrot.

ANGEL ABOVE MY HEAD

by James V. Randazzo

About fourteen years ago Barbara (my wife) came to me with a sheepish gleam in her eye and began a statement with, "Honey, I don't ask for much ..." In my mind she wanted another baby, so when I found out she only wanted to adopt a cat, I offered to drive her to the animal shelter. She showed me a picture in the local newspaper of a female cat that would be destroyed if not adopted by the end of the week. My only warning concerned our other pet, Tigger. He was used to being the top cat and might be very jealous and hateful.

"I'll take that chance," she said, and so a beautiful calico named Angel came into our lives.

Angel lived up to her name, giving unconditional love and tenderness to everyone, even Tigger. Almost every night they would groom each other, and to see them snuggle in front of our fireplace could make even the most callous non-romantic jealous.

Angel was the favorite of family and friends alike, but the bond she and Barbara shared was special. Occasionally when Angel used to take adventures into the neighborhood, I'd joke with the kids that we might as well not come back if Angel wasn't found.

Angel slept most of the time above Barbara's head on her pillow. It reminded me of a Neil Diamond song *Angel Above My Head*, which is an ode to his deceased father.

When Angel fell sick, Barbara was the one who took it the hardest and worked diligently to save her. With the aid of understanding coworkers, she rearranged her work schedule to take consecutive days off in order to follow the vet's orders explicitly.

Now some people don't see the hand of God in animals, but all I know is this animal not only demonstrated unconditional love, it ministered to Barbara. Somehow Angel knew she couldn't just die; she had to prepare Barbara for the loss.

Over the final week, Angel convinced Barbara her time was near. She kept her loving personality and fighting spirit, but stopped eating. After a few days of being force-fed, she even bit Barbara's finger as if to say, "Don't push it, girl. It's time."

One night I awoke around three o'clock to find Barbara comforting Angel. It was almost like they both knew. That day was going to be the last Barbara could take off from her job. I'm sure she thought to herself, "Who will care for Angel while I'm at work?" But it was a problem we didn't have to face. As if she understood our concern, Angel passed away shortly after noon that very day, making sure it was a convenient time and that Barbara had our son, Andrew, there to support her.

Some people may not believe in the power of God in nature, or in the interconnectedness of life. But I do. In the grand scheme of things, our Angel was only a cat. But I feel there were too many loving connections not to believe she was so much more.

To all the children in heaven taken too soon; to all the grandparents in heaven who just need some warmth on their laps, God brought back a real gem; an animal unique among animals. Enjoy every minute with her. We surely did.

Jim Randazzo is a high school science teacher and father of three. From his home in New Jersey, he maintains a website www.onepotatochip.com *which is dedicated to proving the connections between God and mankind. His website's slogan: Every life has a purpose and connection.*

PRINCESS ASHLEY

Phyllis Blakely

SOMETHING GOOD TO BE

by Cullyn Foxlee

A dog runs in a pack
As do we
A cat stands alone
As do we
A rat strives in vain to escape her cage
As do we
A horse follows the wind on a whim
As do we
A pig acquaints himself well with gluttony
As do we
A rabbit has a timid, but painful, bite
As do we
A gerbil arduously goes nowhere
As do we
A turtle hides in his shell
As do we
A snake has a forked tongue
As do we
Yet when any of these animals need assistance
Do we help them?
Certainly
That is why a human is something good
To be

Cullyn Foxlee lives in Sequim, Washington. She has always loved animals and searches for any opportunity to help them. Cullyn was sixteen when she wrote "Something Good to Be."

KITTENS

by Tina Oaks

It was a cold and rainy afternoon, not the proverbial dark and stormy night, that December when I arrived home and heard a distinctive peeping sound. For a minute I tried to convince myself it was a bird, but my instincts told me the pregnant female cat who had been hanging around our house had had her kittens. After putting my purse away, I went searching. It took only a moment to find four cold, wet kittens about five days old in the flower bed. The mom was nowhere to be found.

I couldn't just leave them there, so I got a box and put the kittens in it with a towel. I turned around and there was the mom. She crawled in with her babies and gave me a look of gratitude. I went inside and thought about the situation. With a husband, a home, one cat, three dogs, two jobs and a brand new granddaughter, I didn't have time for this. But I love baby anythings and went back outside to see how they were doing. Lo and behold there was a fifth baby. About half the size of his siblings, he was cold, half dead, and pushed into the corner of the box. I put him next to his mom and figured he'd be dead in the morning, but he survived.

A few days later, it became apparent the mom was just too small to take care of all her babies, so I was elected to fill in. In the meantime the box, kittens and mom had been moved from the front porch to the back porch to the garage and now they were coming into the house. I figured if I had to feed and care for these guys, they may as well be close at hand. By now the kittens had their eyes open and were ready to start exploring with great relish; this was pretty fun, at least for the first few days. The original four were doing okay being taught by a human, with help from their mom, to eat on their own. But the little guy was struggling. He hadn't learned to suckle very well, with his siblings pushing him out of the way. So he and I would sit together, and he would lick milk from my finger. He was very quiet and would sit with me for hours if he could.

All five kittens thrived, and soon it was time for them to go. Friends were told, signs were posted, and one by one they found new homes. We were down to just the little guy when my husband took a call from someone inquiring about the kittens. He told the man they were all gone.

"What?" I asked. "What about the little one?" By now the mom had adopted us, and I didn't want any more cats.

My husband said, "But he's so cute. I thought we would keep him."

So keep him we did. And what a surprise he was. He must have been waiting for all his siblings to leave before showing his true colors. He was extremely busy; opening cupboards, drawers and doors, taking things, tearing up plants, tormenting the other cats and dogs, turning on the microwave, etc. etc. etc. But he and I had bonded during his first few weeks of life, and I was hooked. Besides, he and our granddaughter took a liking to each other. As naughty as he can be sometimes, I love him anyway because he is my little guy.

Born in Port Angeles, Washington, and raised in many western states, Tina Oaks returned to the Olympic Peninsula in 1994 where she now resides with her husband, Doug, and their three rescued cats and two adopted dogs. Tina is a licensed massage practitioner with a business in Port Angeles.

RUCKUS

by Karen Grimsley

Rukus is a yellow lab who is six years old and very fit and energetic. He has been a source of delight and dismay to us (his grandparents) and my daughter, Marci, over the past years. It would take many pages to recite all of his adventures in our family, but one in particular captures the essence of his personality.

Marci and Janet recently bought a large two story house on Vashon Island. A beautiful house on acreage with lots of room for Rukus to run and hopefully use up some of his energy. He seemed to like the change in houses from the city of Seattle because he spent a lot of time exploring the area, smelling new smells and looking for food.

Rukus will eat anything that is left unattended; including some not so edible things such as handles on portable coolers, watermelon rind, cardboard wrappers, deer entrails in the woods, and people's coat pockets (if they'd held a dog cookie at one time). The list of items he has consumed over his lifetime is very long.

Before the sellers moved out of the house, the owner advised Marci that there might be a problem with mice in the laundry room, as a forty pound bag of dog food she had put in that room seemed to be slowly disappearing.

When Marci and Janet were ready to move in, they discovered the house hadn't been thoroughly cleaned. After cleaning the living room, Marci decided to clean the laundry room next. Finding a small opening near the baseboard in the wall, she got the shop vacuum and was able to get at least five pounds of dog food out of the wall. Then she sealed the hole, thus ending the rodent problem. Rukus was very interested in this process.

Later in the day Rukus was nowhere to be found. Janet and Marci searched the property, calling and getting anxious as it was getting dark, and he was still getting used to his new surroundings. Janet decided to check the rooms in the house once again, both upstairs and downstairs. There he was. In the laundry room, sitting very quietly and staring intently at the wall as if to say: "My prayer has been answered. A wall that dispenses dog food. I just have to be patient."

Karen Grimsley is in her 70's. She and her husband have four adult children who were all born in Port Angeles. Growing up, her family had an assortment of family pets, all of whom lived together very happily. They included a tarantula (named Natasha), several goldfish, a turtle (named Oglethorp), pet rats, gerbils, two dogs and a cat. Now her children all have dogs, and when they travel, she and her husband are the trusted dog sitters. This way, she gets her "puppy fix."

4 PAWS AWARD

His Day

by Kevin Torres

They say every dog has his day.

Bernard was half Labrador and half Australian shepherd, with an all-black coat except for some white on his chest. He had been taken from his mother at a young age and was one of the last pups to be picked out of the pound. As he watched all the other dogs being chosen over himself, Bernard refused to lose hope, and every time he saw a new group of excited kids rush in, he would romp to the front of the cage, wagging his tail. After what seemed like an eternity, he was finally picked by a family consisting of two parents and a lone boy of seven.

It was established the first night in his new home that Bernard would sleep on the bed with the boy, and this quickly became something he looked forward to all day long. Almost every night, the boy would hug or pet Bernard to sleep, talking to him gently. Sometimes if the boy was troubled by something, he would tell Bernard his problems, and Bernard would rub his nose on the boy's face or place his head on the boy's lap. This always seemed to make the boy feel better, just as it did Bernard.

Those nights turned into weeks, then months, then years. The boy grew taller and his voice deepened. Bernard began to have trouble running after balls and Frisbees, swimming was now more of a chore than pleasure, and even breathing became an inconvenience at times. But he still had the joy of every night being able to lie at the foot of the boy's bed.

The boy was Bernard's life. Every day when the boy would return from school, Bernard would race to meet him at the door. A loving hug or ear tousle from the boy was enough for Bernard to forget the aches and frustrations of getting older.

Passing years always bring change, and one ordinary day, as Bernard lay in the sunshine next to a window, he heard the front door unlatch. He only opened his left eye, for his right eye was getting hard to see out of, and saw the boy's father walk in holding a cardboard box. At first it didn't seem important, but when the boy's mother and the boy ran to look into the box, Bernard became curious.

It hurt to lift himself to his feet, but he did it and tottered over to peek into the box, which had been placed on the ground. Inside was something he hadn't expected: a puppy. A chubby, bouncy, sleek black Labrador pup.

Why was there a puppy? Bernard turned to the boy for an answer. He stroked the boy's leg with his paw, but the boy didn't even look at Bernard. Instead, the boy picked up the wriggling puppy and held him against his chest. Bernard tried rubbing his head against the boy's leg, but the boy didn't even look down. Not knowing what else to do, Bernard sighed and went back to his spot in the sun, feeling uneasy.

Although Bernard spent the rest of the day in the sunlight, it was as if he was in the shadows. No one even glanced his way; they were all too busy playing with Chester, the energetic new dog.

When it was time to go to sleep, Bernard crept up the stairs. Every step was agony but he continued to climb, knowing that every step got him closer to the boy and the bed he had shared from that first day.

Just as Bernard managed to make it to the top, he heard a shrill bark. It came from the one place Bernard had hoped it wouldn't. Bernard pushed open the boy's half-closed door and stared at a scene straight out of a nightmare. The boy was comforting Chester on his bed. Chester was crying and looked scared, but as the boy soothed him he seemed to feel better. Meanwhile Bernard felt worse and worse. He didn't even notice that the whimpers were no longer coming from Chester, but from himself.

"Hey, Mom," the boy called. "Bernard's making Chester cry. Can you come get him?"

The boy's mother grabbed Bernard by the collar and ushered him out of the room, down the stairs, and into a cot in the corner of the living room. All the lights were turned off and Bernard curled into a ball. For the first time since the pound, Bernard cried himself to sleep. He'd never felt so alone.

Things only got worse. As the days went on, Chester completely took over the bed, leaping gracefully onto the mattress and sprawling across what had always been Bernard's spot. He also had no trouble beating Bernard to the front door when the boy returned from school. Bernard tried getting to the tennis ball before Chester, but was too slow. He could barely run at all, his panting was wheezy, his legs wobbled and his joints popped.

Other than his food bowl always being kept full, it seemed as if Bernard had been forgotten by the whole family. He was hardly ever talked to or petted. The only way he could guarantee that he was even recognized was to lie on top of the boy's lap when he was watching TV. "Down!" and "No!" were the majority of the words he ever heard. He didn't know what to do. Hadn't he always been a good dog?

One morning Bernard woke to the smell of bacon. Feeling hungrier than usual, he stood up and walked painfully into the kitchen. There was the family eating breakfast, with Chester under the table gazing up at the boy with his puppy-dog eyes and wagging tail.

Bernard limped over to his bowl and for the first time found it empty. Looking questioningly over his shoulder, he was just in time to see the boy giving Chester a strip of bacon. Mouth watering, Bernard moved over to the table and put his head on the boy's lap.

The boy looked down. It was the first time Bernard could remember their eyes meeting since Chester had arrived. Bernard watched attentively as the boy reached across the table. To grab a piece of bacon? Bernard's stomach growled as he ran his tongue around his salivating jaws.

But it was not to be. The boy showed Bernard a plate with nothing on it. All the bacon was gone. Bernard's stomach began to hurt more, but not as much as his heart.

Watching Chester happily nibbling his strip of bacon, Bernard decided he'd had enough. The good times were gone, and he was barely an afterthought in the family now. He decided to spend the rest of his short life somewhere else. There was a forest at the edge of the property in the backyard. In silent misery he waited by the sliding door for someone to let him out.

It was the boy who eventually came and opened the door. Bernard gazed up, but the boy didn't seem to notice the sad brown eyes staring up at him with so much hope and adoration.

Bernard hung his head and walked slowly across the patio and into the yard. Every step racked his body with pain. He suspected it wouldn't be long before he wouldn't be able to walk at all.

When he reached the end of the yard, he took one last glance back at the house in which he'd lived for so long, then turned away and hobbled into the woods.

Suddenly Bernard stopped cold. The hair on his body stood up, much like his ears as they picked up an alarming sound. Breaking glass. Screams. Something bad was happening at the house!

Bernard turned and ran as fast as he could back the way he'd come. His body was on fire, the pain was indescribable, but all he could think about was getting to the boy, being there, protecting him.

As Bernard reached the house he saw that the sliding door had been shattered. Inside the kitchen, the boy and his parents crouched on the floor in terror. Above them stood a man in black, pointing a small object at them. Bernard's instincts yelled that this stranger was bad.

He hurtled across the patio, heedless of the shards of glass from the broken door, and leapt full force against the stranger's back. The man lurched forward and Bernard locked his jaws around his throat. The man tried to throw him off, but Bernard wouldn't let go. All he could think of was saving the boy. He wasn't going to stop until he'd made sure he'd done so.

Then came a loud boom. Bernard yelped and slid to a heap on the floor. With his good eye, he watched the boy's father leap up and hit the stranger over the head with a chair, and Bernard knew the boy was safe now.

He closed his eye. It was the only thing he seemed to be able to move.

When he opened it again, he was in an unfamiliar room with a harsh bright light above him. The entire place seemed cold, and he was cold, too. And so weak. He couldn't even whimper.

And then the boy was there.

With tears in his eyes, the boy came to Bernard's side and began to pet him. Warmth spread throughout Bernard's body, erasing the dreadful cold.

"Oh Bernard," said the boy. "You are the best dog in the world!"

Bernard watched as for the first time the boy laid at the foot of *his* bed instead of the other way around. Bernard knew that this was the end, but never in his long life had he felt so good.

This was his day.

Kevin Torres is a senior at Sequim High School and enjoys writing as a hobby. His dog, Shadow, is his best friend.

PLEASE COME BACK

Dee Smiley

4 PAWS AWARD

RESCUE ME

by Joe Wright

A sweet little life, abandoned and scared
Left on the road, by no one who cared

Left in the desert, left there to die
Left with her sister, both meek and shy

A sweet little puppy, with feet sore and raw
Whose abuse included being burnt on each paw

Innocent victims of the cruelty of man
Thrown from a car, a truck, or a van

Left without water, no help for their thirst
Left without food, the puppies were cursed

These sweet little creatures, filled with trust and with love
Are God's special gifts, gifts from above
And though there is cruelty, there are many who care
People who rescue, from here and from there

So let's hear some praise, and let's hear a cheer
For the people who rescue these babies so dear

Joe Wright is the regional manager for a trade show service company. Poetry is one of his hobbies when time permits. Joe and his wife Robyn live in Clackamas, Oregon, with their dogs, who were all rescued.

CALL ME ANTHROPOMORPHIC

by Deborah Daline

Pia came to me out of the untimely death of a friend. In the shock, sadness and confusion after my friend's death, his two cats somehow were lost. At the time I had an amazing, elderly, domineering, part-Maine coon cat by the name of Amy. I adored her, but knew she would not abide another feline in her kingdom. After several weeks the thought of those two cats in the wild still haunted me. Finally, one afternoon, I packed my old Honda with a cage, heavy gloves, and a can of Amy's favorite cat food. She would have been furious if she'd realized what I was doing.

Would being a couple help them survive? I wondered as I went to rescue the pair. Not against a pack of coyotes. One of the cats was sleek, black, with an exotic-sounding name, impossible to remember. The other was an uncategorizable cat called Pia. I had vague plans about what to with them once I captured the duo. I figured it would be fairly easy to find a home for the black one, but didn't know if anyone would fall for Pia.

I did dread going to my friend's empty house, and first asked all the neighbors if they had seen the cats. One neighbor said she had left food out and thought she had seen Pia. This gave me hope. I walked around the forlorn house, holding the can of cat food and calling her name. She came to me immediately. No need for cat food, no need for a cage, no need for gloves. All she wanted was the touch of a human hand.

I put Pia in the car and continued to call for her partner. I called as long as I could that day. I came back several more times and called. The black cat didn't come. I stopped calling for her just about the time I stopped crying for my friend. At that point, an image came to me. Just as I pictured my friend in a better place,

I pictured the black cat sitting on a satin pillow being served sardines in a crystal bowl. It was time to let go.

I cleaned my back shed and created a cozy sleeping place for Pia. I filled bowls of food and water and attached a sign on the door proclaiming "Pia's Place." Silly, as if she could read. I kept her in there for a while, visiting often. On one such occasion after I opened the door, she ran outside and into Amy. There was much posturing and growling, but, to my surprise, no attacks. Amy was very old and wise; she wouldn't win a fight with this almost wildcat. And Pia was smart too, deferring to the resident cat.

The summer passed, and as the weather changed, I decided to see if the shed-cat could come in from the cold. I kept her in the back room with the door closed. This was a catchall space, but also contained a futon for summer guests. Pia seemed content. Time passed, and we were into winter. The back room wasn't heated. One day, I left the door open and Pia ventured out into the kitchen. She came into the room along the edges. She sniffed Amy's food bowls. Amy sat on the settee by the crackling wood stove and didn't seem to notice her. She was twenty-something and her senses not so sharp, I thought.

And so it continued, Pia slinking around the perimeters of rooms and sitting perfectly still, a statue, if Amy happened to glance her way. It seemed a sort of game: Amy pretending Pia didn't exist and Pia happily playing along. One day, of course, they bumped into each other. Amy hissed and lashed out. Pia froze, then fled. And after that, as if the catfrontation was forgotten, the game continued complete with an occasional Amy hissy fit.

Spring came and Amy was willing to go out and sit in the sun on the side step. Pia went out the back room window to her sun spot. Amy didn't intrude on Pia's spot, and Pia didn't intrude on Amy's, so it worked. It seems they must have split up the outside territory as well. Besides the side step Amy spent much time sitting in a dignified manner under the mock orange. Pia preferred to sprawl among the wildflowers.

Later in the summer I made Amy a crown of dandelions and took a picture. Then one warm August day, she disappeared. I searched the yard, crawled under the house, and canvassed the neighborhood. I posted her picture with the dandelion crown on a telephone pole. The animal shelter was given a detailed description. I asked Pia where Amy was, as if she would tell me even if she could.

Days passed. Weeks passed. And during this time, Pia became bolder. She came out from the edges and walked through the middle of rooms. She sat on the step by the side door. It was like the invisible cat coming into view, with all her delightful details. She has a caramel-colored spot on her chin; she has a right back foot that kicks uncontrollably; she cocks her head when looking at something interesting; and she snorts in her sleep. What she loves more than anything else, more than a can of gourmet cat food, is the touch of a human hand. But not any hand, only mine. During that time of looking for Amy, I fell in love with Pia. Then Amy came back.

Neither of us could believe it. We were sitting on the side steps one morning, and Amy came through the gate. She was emaciated and her fur hung in tangles. She was so weak she could barely walk. She looked at Pia and me on the steps accusingly.

"Amy," I whispered, and Pia cocked her head. Then, she walked towards Amy, straight towards her. Amy stood shakily still. Pia walked closer and closer, and I held my breath. Would she assert her newfound status? Neither one of them made a sound, and then Pia touched her nose to Amy's. It was one of the kindest acts I've ever witnessed, and between two animals. Consider: how many humans would react so sweetly under similar circumstances?

After Amy's return, their relationship didn't change much. Amy continued to hiss if Pia came too close, but as summer turned to autumn and on to winter, Amy continued to weaken. I found her one morning, sitting on the settee by the fire, a body without a spirit. I buried her under the mock orange on a rainy day. Pia watched, standing at a respectful distance. At least that's how it seemed.

Now, Pia is the cat of the house and brings me presents of large rats. I look into her complex eyes and see a survivor. She is paradoxical: brave and cautious. Her claws are sharp and her paws are soft. I found her in a time of sorrow, and she's given me much happiness. She's an ordinary cat who showed me an extraordinary moment of what I can only call compassion for a fellow cat. Call me anthropomorphic, I don't care. I've said it before, but I'll say it again, more specifically: if people could be more like my cat, Pia, it would be a better planet.

Deborah Daline is a writer who works part time as an educational assistant in Port Townsend schools. Summers, her house is a "private getaway," where guests are "vetted" by her cat, Pia.

MAX AND BANDIT

by Beverlee Benbow

Written in memory of two wonderful dogs.

With sleepy eyes, I opened the kitchen door to let my Brittany Spaniels, Max and Bandit, outside for their morning constitutional. In the moonless morning, my husband's headlights reflected off the deep snow-covered ground, as I watched him slowly drive up the hill on his way to work.

I turned the porch light on and gasped in surprise. Standing five feet in front of me was a towering moose with only the deck railing separating us. For a moment we both seemed apprehensive; she looked at me, and I looked at her. All I could think was: *Who is going to back off first?*

I glanced down at my dogs, and like me, they appeared to be in shock. When the animal, twenty times their size, moved her head, they started to bark defensively. Since an irritated moose will react like a bronco out of a rodeo chute, I grabbed my dogs by their collars and pulled them back inside the house.

As the sun rose, I waited patiently for the moose to meander up the road so my poor dogs could go outside. Another hour passed, and she didn't show any inclination to want to leave the yard. In fact, she appeared to enjoy eating twigs off our Choke Cherry tree, reshaping it as she browsed.

I had given that tree to my husband for a gift years before, and transplanted it from our old residence to our new home. Fearing the moose would devour the young tree, I called my husband at work for his advice.

"Turn the dogs on her," he said.

I was hoping he could think of another solution. Pitting animals against each other seems as barbaric as a cockfight. On the other hand, we'd spent five years babying and pruning our precious Choke Cherry tree.

Since husbands, supposedly, retain a status for being wise, I opened the door and said, "Go get her."

The inspired-barking dogs charged out the door after the moose. The startled moose backed off from the tree, ran about thirty feet towards the end of our yard, made a sharp turn, lowered her head, laid back her ears, and I said, "Oh sh—!" With visions of her kicking and stomping my dogs to death, I called them back to the kitchen door.

Thankfully, Max and Bandit returned on my command. I credit their reaction to hours of me teaching them commands.

Refusing to retreat, our moose made herself quite at home, lying down in our yard. Occasionally, she glanced over at me through our kitchen window with what I can only describe as a defiant look.

My dogs still needed to be let outside. I led the dogs downstairs through the garage to the outside. The moose couldn't see the dogs exiting the garage and wasn't intimidated by the sound of the automatic garage door opener.

As the day wore on, I watched the dogs make peace with the dominating female. Showing no fear of being kicked, Max and Bandit escorted the moose around our frozen yard. By evening, the moose left the yard, and my husband returned.

He cut ice blocks and constructed a five foot wall around the tree. If the moose returned, he wanted to redirect her to the Willow behind our house. We were not only trying to save the shape of our tree, but her life as well. Every year, moose die from starvation, but with full stomachs. Moose have a limited diet that nature provides. Hay, garden vegetables, and flowers give no nutritional value.

The next day she was back, stretching her head past the top of the ice wall, munching on the edges of the dried up cherry stems. Oddly enough, I wanted to applaud her; she was 1000 pounds of determination. Plus she had made friends with one cantankerous Spaniel named Bandit and a sweet-natured dog named Max.

That day I realized, left to themselves, wild and domesticated animals learn to live in harmony, but with self-imposed limits. The fact that the female didn't have a calf to protect permitted the animals to find a common bond and walk side by side. If animals can find common ground, then humans should be able to do the same.

Max and Bandit were discards from a breeder. Beverlee found them at an animal shelter recommended by her veterinarian. Since she's "an old softie," she couldn't separate the boys. She planned for one dog and ended up with two!

4 PAWS AWARD
Historical Critters

DOGS OF MY CHILDHOOD

by Barbara Pelett

In 1950 my mother, my sister and I lived in Bremerton, Washington, in a tiny house on a dirt road with a view of an island in Oyster Bay. My dad had served in the army in Europe, but he was gone. Our neighborhood was made up of modest homes and woods. Beyond the woods was an abandoned trailer park and a couple of empty cabins—housing that was necessary when the naval shipyard was going full steam during "The War," but empty ever since.

Most people thought of their dogs differently then. Drop them off near "a good home" when you didn't want them anymore. Spaying was for rich folks; feed them leftovers; no shots; all dogs had fleas; most dogs chased cars.

I must have been about nine when a "wild" dog hit my radar screen. She lived under one of the empty cabins with her pup who had clearly been fathered by my dog Cubby. She was a small shepherd sort of dog with a red coat. Her pup was red and roly-poly with Cubby's stubby tail. I heard that the cabin owner planned to shoot the dogs so I formed a half-baked plan to save the puppy.

Over the course of a week I lay on my stomach on the cabin porch tempting him with meaty tidbits until he was close enough to grab. I snatched him up, hauled him home and put a little harness on him with a rope. As soon as I set him down, he hightailed it back up the hill to his mother's den—yip, yip, yipping, with me on the end of the rope. At the cabin I gathered him up again, took him back, and his mom followed. I shut them in the basement and fed them. That's where my mother found them when she got home from work. The next day I began to look for homes for them.

They were pretty dogs, so within a few days I'd found new owners for each of them a little farther out Marine Drive, the peninsula we lived on that formed Oyster Bay. The pup was closest; the mom was about a mile away.

She was back at our door the next day. She brought the pup with her. I returned them to their new homes, but the next morning she was back again with her pup. This time she was dragging a twenty-foot chain.

We admitted to ourselves that we'd been "chosen" by the mama dog, and named her Trouble. The pup went to his permanent home with no further problem.

The phase of our lives when my mother was called "The Dog Lady" began. You see, Trouble had lived under that house long enough to have two batches of puppies. A female survived from the first litter. She was red like her mother, but had slick hair. She was born wild, lived well, and never took up domestic life with humans. She hung out near her mother, Trouble, but she never came within arm's length of us. We called her Sis.

Every summer each dog had pups about three weeks apart. Trouble's puppies were easy. They were generally born in our kitchen. Sis, however, grew increasingly clever at hiding hers. The most challenging was the year she put her den in the middle of a large patch of Himalayan blackberries.

Sis was a dog of about thirty pounds. I was still in grade school, small enough to crawl on my belly and elbows through her tunnel in the brambles. I waited until it was time for the pups to be weaned, then crawled into the thicket, took one pup at a time and wriggled out backwards. She never challenged me.

Occasionally we found homes for the pups. For the most part though, they went to the pet store in downtown Bremerton for free. At the pet store they sold for about $5 each. One year we had eighteen dogs briefly—three "regulars" and fifteen pups.

You already know Trouble. I've mentioned Cubby briefly, the one time he was probably the father of one of Trouble's pups. The last permanent dog was Bruno. I say "permanent," but that's not entirely true. Bruno showed up one day—a mature shepherd mix with a white ruff and a wise face. He looked like someone's grandpa who had just told a joke. He was mellow; he made beautiful pups; and he disappeared every summer.

As I got a little older, I traveled a little farther away from home myself. One summer I made my way to Lower Marine Drive where rich people lived on low-bank waterfront. There was Bruno, hanging at the beach and going by the name of "Bum."

Bruno never missed his fatherly duties in spite of his other persona. We always felt flattered that he died in the winter while staying at our house.

After that, the quality of the puppies went downhill. A good-sized Airedale took up residence in our woods. We called him Arthur. We were able to keep Trouble away from him, but Sis was incorrigible. No more shepherd markings; instead, grizzled whiskers on puppy faces. Still, we were giving them away for free, and the pet store always managed to sell them.

Arthur and Sis appeared to live well. No one was giving them any sort of vet services, but they were sleek and their coats were shiny. Somehow they seemed well fed. Once, just once, my sister was walking in the woods and Arthur approached her. He wasn't a scary dog, so she wasn't afraid. For reasons of his own, Arthur put both his front paws on her shoulders and looked her full in the face, then flitted away.

I'd like to tell you how these wild dogs made out, but I can't. When I was fourteen, my mother had to sell our house, and we moved in with my grandparents on the other side of the Bay. Trouble, of course, came with us. Bruno and Cubby were gone by then. I'd like to think that Sis and Arthur continued to thrive in their own mysterious ways. Perhaps it's true.

Barbara Pelett is retired from the Oregon Liquor Control Commission. She lives in Port Angeles, Washington with husband, Tom, and two rescued dogs, Bosley and Connor. Connor is the second dog the Peletts have adopted from PFOA.

4 PAWS AWARD

Summer "Inspurration"

by Mary Margolis

Cinnamon colored noses
Leave prints on dusty windows
Eyes slit in the sunlight
Pupils like watermelon seeds
Soft mews begging
To join me outside
Purrs reminding me to
Enjoy each moment
To be inspired by birds, jays, robins
Children's laughter
The joy of blooming flowers in
Reds, yellows, whites;
roses, lilies, daisies,
Each shade brilliant against
The blue sky above

Mary Margolis is a freelance writer who has lived in Port Angeles, Washington, since 1990. She is a lifelong cat lover and shares her residence with three fantastic felines. She has been a member and volunteer at Peninsula Friends of Animals for three years. Ms. Margolis also enjoys gardening, beachcombing, reading, and exploring the Olympic Peninsula.

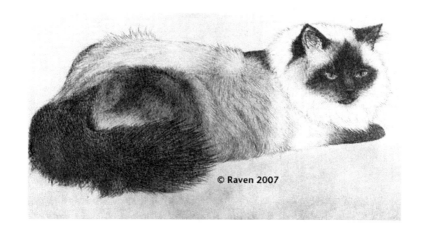

© Raven 2007

BUTTONS

Raven O'Keefe

4 PAWS AWARD

THE THINGS THAT DON'T REALLY MATTER

by Diane Lopez

The windowpane was cold, and Juanita felt its chill on her nose and forehead as she leaned against the glass. With her fingers, she traced the raindrops on their winding paths down the pane, each drop splattering when it hit the windowsill. She noticed, with little alarm, the dirt that each tiny crystal carried along with it, showing that her chore of the day before had not been done as well as it should have been.

What does it matter anyway? she thought, shifting her weight to her other foot. *Nothing matters when it rains. Rain makes everything ugly!*

Juanita knew she was acting childish and not at all like the eleven-year-old she was. *But I can't help it!* she thought, once again becoming aware of the lump in her throat. That awful lump; it had come when she'd first seen the sad stray—the dog now curled between two trash cans at the back of the yard. Early that morning he had slipped through the hedges looking for refuge from the rain, and Juanita had watched as he moved from one corner to another when the cold wind changed direction. She wasn't sure which he was trying to hide from, the wind or the rain. "What does it matter," she murmured out loud, wondering how many times she'd used those same words this morning.

"Juanita, what are you doing out there? Why are you so quiet?" This came from the kitchen where her mother was making a chocolate cake that had the entire house smelling like warm fudge. "If you're still at that window, get away before you smear it."

"Okay, Mom," Juanita answered, making no attempt to move. The dog had just stood up again. This time he walked towards the corner of the back steps just below the window where she was standing. He was a homely animal, his dirty, shaggy coat soaked through. He was shivering, and so thin that each of his ribs could easily be traced. She watched him settle down again, heave a great sigh that shook his entire body, quiver a bit, and close his eyes, safe for the moment from the wind if not the rain.

This time the lump in her throat rose higher, and a tear glistened on her cheek. Although usually sensitive and compassionate, she had never felt such an ache of pity for anything before.

It had begun that morning. She'd come down for breakfast and was told the trip to the zoo would have to be postponed until another day. "This weather's unfit for a dog," her mother explained.

It was a few hours later when, pressing her nose against the windowpane and waiting for the rain to stop, Juanita saw the dog move timidly into the yard. She remained at the window all morning, the zoo entirely forgotten, wishing only that the rain would stop and the warm sun dry the pitiful creature outside. She had turned from the window only once, and that was to ask her mother if she could "bring in that dog out there, just until the rain stops?"

"Oh really, Juanita," her mother replied. "I just scrubbed the floors. Anyway, rain doesn't really matter to him. He's used to it. Besides," she added, "you'll never get rid of him once you're nice to him."

Juanita had wanted to ask which dog the weather wasn't fit for, but she couldn't because of that awful lump in her throat. She could only look outside and say nothing.

"The rain will stop," she heard her mother say. "Now get away from the window." But Juanita had stayed and watched the dog all afternoon as he sighed and shivered, his every movement making her own misery grow deeper.

Her mother came in from the kitchen. "Juanita, why are you moping at the window? I told you, we'll go to the zoo next weekend. Now, how about some cake?"

As the dog gave a great sigh and quivered once more, a chill ran up and down Juanita's arms, and tears blurred her eyes. "I guess it really doesn't matter anyway," she said, crying as she turned her face towards the kitchen and the piece of cake she knew she couldn't eat.

"Come on, honey," her mother coaxed, becoming concerned about her daughter's reluctance to leave the window. "It's chocolate fudge. Your favorite."

"No thank you," Juanita said, swallowing a sob. "I'm not hungry." And she resumed watching the stray.

"My goodness," Juanita's mother exclaimed. "You're not sulking about the zoo, are you? You're worried sick about that dog.

"Poor child," she murmured as she headed to the back door. After a moment, she opened the door and peered down at the stray, feeling cold from the icy rain now blowing in the direction of the steps. "Come on, pooch. I guess we can make room for you."

But the dog didn't stir. With her shoe, she gently poked the back end of the animal, but he lay there, soaking rain running off his fur, his eyes closed. He didn't move, not even the sides of his skinny chest.

"No, Juanita," she whispered. "It doesn't matter now." Then she closed the door, feeling colder than the wind as she took the sobbing child into her arms.

Diane Lopez started volunteering for PFOA as soon as she retired from her career as a school counselor four years ago. She and her husband came to Sequim in 1988 from the east coast. They have a dog, three cats and a pond full of large koi.

Precarious Beginnings

by Ann Chang

My shiny fluffy black cat is named "Bear" because he looks just like a little bear cub when he furs up for the winter. But he might better have been given the name "Rocky" or "Shaky" for the start he got in life. You see, when Bear was tiny—perhaps four weeks old—he was found inside a quart canning jar behind a freezer in a cold garage in the middle of winter. He'd evidently lost his mother and any siblings there might've been, and was crying from hunger, cold, loneliness and desperation. He was truly in a pickle although there were none in that jar—just one mad sad wisp of mewing fur.

I was able to pull him out of the jar and quickly took him into the house where I made my first mistake in his upbringing. I gave him warm milk, which he devoured but which my daughter told me later was not good for him. He should have had milk replacer. Well, he survived the night in spite of me and the next day I suggested to the wise one that she take him to her house and give him milk replacer since she had more time than I did. Little did she know she would be getting up every two hours to feed him!

After trips to the vet for a checkup and an eye infection, Bear grew big and healthy and full of energy. He soon became so feisty with my daughter's cats that she decided it was time for him to move on. So, off he went to the house in town where two of my other children lived. Being on a busy street, they didn't let him outside, which really rumpled his fur. He would pace from windowsill to windowsill, eyeing birds and the great outdoors, and became quite daredevilish in search of excitement. His favorite thing was to take a flying leap at a wall when one of the kids would shine a laser pointer at it. This may be why he's a few kibbles short of a sack of cat food!

One time his recklessness got him into big trouble, necessitating another trip to the vet. My daughter left for work early one morning, and when my son came downstairs there was Bear with white string coming from both ends. Thinking that didn't look right, my son pulled gently on the mouth end of the string, prompting much loud mewing and howling. At the clinic, the vet first made sure there wasn't a needle attached to the string, then gave Bear some "I don't care" medicine and pulled the string out. Bear was quite the celebrity for that day, although an expensive one.

Well, time passes and things change and my daughter went off to college so my son got an apartment for himself and, of course, Bear. Special dispensations and heavy damage deposits later found them living—but not so happily—ever after. The apartment was on the second floor and Bear, still resentful of being cooped up, learned the trick of taking death-defying leaps from my son's deck over ten feet to the deck next door. The neighbors really didn't care for cats, so he had to come back by the same route.

But the habit which finally got him evicted was his penchant for "playful" attacks on my son's fish tank. The aerator got his full attention; he would slap at it with a paw, sloshing water all over the carpet. Not a good thing, in a brand new apartment. My son could have lost his happy home, lock, stock and fish tank, so it was decided that Bear should come back to live with me.

Since my house is near a major highway I was concerned for his safety, but as soon as Bear arrived he made a beeline for the fence and sharpened his claws, as if to mark out his territory, and he has never gone near the road. He is truly happy outdoors, where he can hunt and prowl and be king of that world.

My bear cat is now seven years old, a champion mouser with a royal attitude. He's survived well in spite of his perilous beginnings, several homes, and many adventures. He's never been a cheap date, but he's also never given his people-family a dull moment. Is he spoiled? Yes. Is he a special cat? Yes.

And now he's home for good.

Ann Chang is a healthcare worker who has always been "happily owned" by her pets!! She lives in Port Angeles, Washington, with her husband and her cat, Bear.

© Raven 2007

Ian & Moss

Raven O'Keefe

MY SHELTER DOG

by Terry Metheny

I once read a book on making money, or being effective, or was it about influencing people? The author claimed you could learn a lot about dealing with people by noticing how a dog makes its living. It claimed that most dogs don't do much anymore, like herding, or hunting, or guarding, but instead make their living by just being a person's friend. It pointed out that the dog always gets excited when its master returns and is overjoyed at the mere presence of its owner. When its master returns, it never yawns and says, "What? You again?" I guess the author had never met my shelter dog.

I was talking with a couple of good friends and said, "I've been reading up on dogs lately. Did you know that dogs started associating with humans twelve thousand years ago? We started becoming civilized ten thousand years ago, so it only took two thousand years for dogs to whip us into shape. There have been a lot of theories why we've become civilized—warfare, changing climate, food supply. But I know the real reason—that damn dog needed a fireplace to sleep in front of!" They both roared with laughter.

Dogs' influence on human history has been little noted. I suppose because a human having a dog is so common. Nonetheless, all the great military men invariably had dogs. Fredrick the Great of Prussia, who took on the combined efforts of France, Sweden, Russia, Austria and the Holy Roman Empire during the Seven Years War, was a great lover of dogs. Most folks don't know much about him, but they do know one of his quips: "The more I know of men, the more I like dogs!"

I'm an honorary Lt. Colonel. I think the guy who bestowed that on me did so because I'd make statements like: "The first duty of an officer is to earn the undying loyalty of his troops." A lot of ignorant folks think it's about demanding respect. But respect can't be demanded; it has to be earned. This my shelter dog has made abundantly clear to me. I suspect I'm not alone in that realization.

George Washington was a big lover of dogs. The American foxhound breed is largely a result of his efforts. There have been many theories as to why General Washington's army eventually beat the larger and better British Army. But there's only one reason that makes sense to me—he loved dogs. Washington's first campaign was the liberation of Boston, where he succeeded. But his second campaign was the defense of New York, where he lost many battles. What has been little noted was that after losing the Battle of White Plains, one of his soldiers discovered a small dog wandering through no-man's land. It wore a chain and metal nameplate inscribed with the letters "G Howe." The soldier thought this referred to General Howe, the commander of the opposing British Army, and brought the dog to General Washington. Washington's officers wanted to use the dog as a mascot to inspire the American troops. General George thought differently. He waved the white truce flag and had the dog returned to General Howe. In his diary General Howe noted in regards to the incident that General Washington was obviously "a fine gentleman." General Howe beat Washington many more times in battle but allowed Washington's army to make an orderly retreat from every battle rather than pursuing and destroying them. Eventually General Howe's lack of viciousness caused his dismissal and his replacement by the very inferior Cornwallis, who allowed his troops to be trapped at Yorktown. And thus our nation was born; all because of a "fine gentleman" who felt returning a dog to its rightful owner was a greater good.

Many folks have heard of Lewis and Clark. Lately the role of Sacagawea has come to light. Yet what has been little acknowledged is the role of Lewis' big Newfoundland, Seaman, which was immaculately disciplined just like its owner. Like many young women, Sacagawea delighted in commanding the big powerful dog and insisted on taking him with her whenever she met a new tribe of Native Americans. The effect on the Indians she met of this small, frail, seventeen-year-old girl having a hundred and fifty pound plus dog obey her every command must have emphasized her mystical power, for dogs that big were entirely unknown in North America before the arrival of the Europeans. The girl had some mojo.

Perhaps the only thing more powerful than a purchased dog is a shelter dog. That's been my experience anyway. My shelter dog actually came from a good friend who is basically a pet-rescuing machine. She rescues a couple dogs or cats per week on her own and still finds time to devote a day each week to one of the local rescue shelters down in Northern California where she lives and is a full time park ranger. My shelter dog, Auggie Doggie, came my way when he refused to integrate peaceably into her pack of animals.

The brain has eight levels of functioning, four above normal consciousness, and four that comprise normal human consciousness. The first level is infant intelligence, and it works on the forward/backward polarity. Basically it is the part of the brain that says go toward pleasure and away from pain. Opiates like heroin will kick in this type of thinking, and that's why heroin addicts have a tendency to baby talk. The second level of the brain works on the up/down polarity, and it's the predatory mind. It views the world in terms of dominance and submission, and alcohol will kick in this type of thinking. This is the part of consciousness that dominates the typical dog mind. Dog intelligence is divided into three categories: instinctive, adaptive and obedience. The instinctive mind is where the dog's natural tendencies arise. The adaptive mind is essentially the problem-solving intelligence. The obedience intelligence is the desire to please. It is interesting to note that the higher the obedience intelligence, the lower the adaptive intelligence, and vice versa. It makes sense in that the adaptive intelligence gives the dog the ability to survive in the wild, and a dog that can't survive in the wild would be well advised to find a human and do its damnedest to please him.

My shelter dog, Auggie, has an incredible adaptive intelligence. That's why he's so noncommittal toward humans. He could get along without us. As a matter of fact, based on my observations, he spent a significant amount of time doing exactly that as a homeless dog. He also has a very high need for dominance. I took him to the Sequim dog park a couple weeks ago, and he insisted on growling at a hundred and forty pound Husky. Auggie's about eighty pounds. It wasn't a threatening growl; just one that said, "Hey, I'm the boss around here."

Of course, all kinds of dogs can end up in shelters. But my pet-rescuing machine friend tells me that Auggie is a good representative of the kind of dog that ends up in shelters and is never adopted; older males with high dominance and low obedience. In a word, they are "problem" dogs because they aren't easy to train or easy to handle. My friend adopted Auggie because he'd been in the no-kill shelter the longest, about two years. The shelter owner made it clear that Auggie was a loser because he was never going to be adopted, and that feeding and taking care of him was a waste. She fell for the bait and took him home only to find he was too much to handle. If my friend is a pet-rescuing machine, I'm a problem-solving machine. I love solving problems and am currently working on combining theoretical physics with contextual metaphysics and human psychology. Call it the unified knowledge field theory. I call it "alchemy." So I found

Auggie to be a perfect test subject. When I got him he was a horrible fence-fighter; he attacked every dog he could. He wanted to be walked at least six hours a day and whined when he didn't get his way. He chewed things up if he was left alone and stole food off the counters whenever possible. Two years later I get compliments on his good behavior about once a week! It hasn't been an easy road. But what I've given him doesn't come anywhere near close to what I've received from him. I've greatly increased my self-discipline, patience, stick-with-it-ness, self-esteem, understanding of dominance and submission in both dogs and humans, knowledge of human history, and I've lost my fear of dogs.

I've always taken physical fitness to be of paramount importance, mostly because in my twenties I read about a study that found 95% of folks came down with a major health complication twenty years after they stopped exercising. The Harvard medical school said something about a decade ago that kind of parallels this idea. They found there is really no such thing as aging, just the desire for greater and greater inactivity. The longest-lived human made it to a hundred and twenty-two years. The longest-lived dog made it twenty-nine years. That's two hundred and ten in human years! I hope you laughed at that, because it's a joke. If you do the math properly, dog years to human years are closer to four to one than the seven to one that's so blithely and self-servingly quoted. Dogs are no different from people: without exercise they die young. When I was forty-five I realized I was never going to run again. I had lost the desire and stopped doing it at about forty. My hips had begun to hurt, and I just couldn't trust them anymore. After walking that stupid Auggie for a year and many miles a day, I found short bursts of running possible. I enjoy walking a dog off the leash, but given Auggie's high independence this was always a risky practice. One thing about the dog mind that is abundantly clear is: if the dog's in front, it's the leader. Auggie has no trouble following me off the leash when I'm in front of him. All I have to do is earn the right by running my rear off. And guess what. I can run again.

But that's not the greatest gift Auggie has given me, not by far. After I had him about a year, I realized that while we'd come a long way together in terms of behavior, we really weren't that close. I read a book on dogs about that time which claimed you could increase the bonding between dog and human by rubbing the dog's chest and belly or by rubbing its lower back. At this time Auggie was sleeping on a couch in the front room. On my way back from the bathroom in the middle of the night I began to ambush him with a good dose of belly rubbing while he slept. After a week of these ambushes, I noticed that when I'd walk by him in the middle of the night, he'd roll onto his back, crook his little forepaws and splay his back legs in a position of complete vulnerability and completely unbecoming of such a dominant dog. The sight of his dark silhouette began to make me laugh. He would certainly never do such a thing when he was fully awake. I began to appreciate the little puppy inside that he tried so hard to hide when he was more in control and more reserved.

Recently I took Auggie down to see Emily, the pet-rescuing machine. She marveled at the changed dog that stood before her and said, "Now I know I did give him to the right person." All I could say was thank you, not for giving me the opportunity to show what a good problem-solving person I am, but for something far greater.

I used to think that I'd loved before, but I had no idea what love really is. See, my idea of love was based on the premise that the other being had to deserve my love. But what Auggie taught me is that love is the other way around: it is the giving of love that makes me deserve love. And that's the greatest gift a person can get, and one that is available with a shelter dog.

Terry Metheny is a freelance nature writer from California who currently resides in Port Angeles to care for his mother. He has a BA in English Literature with honors from UC Santa Cruz. Auggie is doing well and is well loved by many in the community.

MATT'S CAT

by Vern Ward

Matt has a cat
Matt's cat is fat, fat, fat
Matt is twice as fat as his cat

Vern Ward is a member of the Muckleshoot Tribe. He has lived in LaPush for most of his life. Vern is thoughtful and caring. His writing reflects his humor and sensitivity. He is currently a student at the Quileute Tribal School in LaPush.

BLUE CAT

Ali Seeber-Lestage

4 PAWS AWARD
Best Fiction

THE IRISH CAT

by Ann Gilson

O'Malley was a middle-aged tomcat, or had been until he came to live with Mrs. Scroggins. She had no truck with fighting and looking for willing lady cats at night, when any respectable cat should be at home in front of the fire. So after a trip to Dr. Grimm, O'Malley lost interest in fights and ladies, and enjoyed the comforts of the fireside with Mrs. Scroggins.

O'Malley was Irish on his father's side—his father having been a ginger colored immigrant who'd stowed away on a ship that had anchored at an Irish port many years ago. O'Malley didn't know this, not having had the honor of his father's acquaintance.

His conception had been the result of his mother's slipping away through an unscreened window one night when she was young, an event her owners saw to it never happened again. O'Malley, in his youth, sneaked out that same window and never returned, preferring to roam, as his father had before him.

After several years of roaming and a couple of years with Mrs. Scroggins, O'Malley felt that he'd seen and done it all, and that life held no more surprises but would go along pretty much the same from now on.

That was before the little green man dropped in to see him one night. Mrs. Scroggins had set out a saucer of half-and-half for O'Malley before going to bed. O'Malley had drunk it, washed his paws, chin and whiskers carefully, and had disposed himself comfortably in the window-seat where he could keep an eye on the dying fire and yet see out onto the moonlit lawn where an early frost rimed the bushes and the walks.

He was just about to doze off when a little green man, clad also in green, with a green pointed hat and shoes with long pointed toes, walked through the window and sat down at the other end of the window-seat, facing him. O'Malley blinked, sure his eyes were deceiving him. But no, the window was still firmly closed and locked—the little man had walked right through it.

Neither one said anything at first, just looked at each other, with the moonlight pouring down over them and striking a glint in each set of eyes.

"O'Malley, I need your help," the little man finally said. He didn't say it in English, or Irish either for that matter. His tinny little voice spoke O'Malley's own language, right inside his head, just as all cats speak to each other.

O'Malley sat up and asked, "Why, what has happened? Why do you need me?"

So the little green man told his story. His race was historically believed to mostly play tricks on people, and sometimes even to cause troubles, but as he told O'Malley, this was to disguise their real purpose, which was to guide and protect Irish cats. Sometimes they *did* play tricks on people, but only to help cats, or to pay back people who were threatening their welfare.

This particular little green fellow had been assigned to O'Malley's father and had done his best by him, though the cat had been opposed to any guidance and was as foolhardy as they came. He was always dashing in where angels fear to tread and generally acting as if there were no tomorrow.

"Indeed," the little man said, "He's come close to being the death of us both more than once. And now, he's surely going to meet his own death if you don't help me."

"All right," said O'Malley. "What do you want me to do? Where is he?"

"He's in the trash dumpster behind Safeway, about three blocks east of here," replied the little man, "and the trash truck will be coming in about a half hour. If he's still in it when it's tipped in and compacted, that's the end of him."

"What in the world is he doing in *there*?" asked O'Malley, fastidiously wrinkling his nose.

"Well, the meat cutter came out and tossed some nice steaks, slightly ripe, just the way your father likes them, in the dumpster. Your father was going by, so he stopped and waited in the shadows. When the next person came out and put something in, she left the lid up. So your father dived in and grabbed a steak. He was about to climb out when the meat cutter came back, dropped in a heavy bucket of something, and put the lid down. Your father hasn't moved since—he's out cold."

"Well, what can *I* do?" asked O'Malley. "The house is locked for the night, and even if I were there at Safeway, how could I help my father?"

"I can open the window latch here," said the little man, "but I can't get the dumpster lid open by myself or pull your father out—he weighs more than I do. But between us, I think we can."

So the little man tugged and pulled on the window latch until it gave way. He opened the window, and they both dropped to the ground and headed down the street in the moonlight.

Without a sound, they slipped into the wide alley behind Safeway and approached the big, dark green dumpster. There was still no sound or word from the cat within, though the little man called with his mind.

So O'Malley stretched as tall as he could, and the little man climbed onto his shoulders and pushed and pushed at the heavy plastic lid. He was tremendously strong for his size, and O'Malley had all he could do not to collapse under him. Finally, with one last heave, the top flew back and the little man climbed down.

He walked through the side of the dumpster, and O'Malley leaped up to the rim of the dumpster and down into it to meet him. There, beside them in all the garbage, lay O'Malley's ginger colored father, still clutching the steak he'd been holding in his teeth when he was hit by the bucket.

"Now what?" asked O'Malley.

"Well, I'll tell you what. Let's get this steak away from him and then you get him by the back of the neck like he was a kitten and you were his mother."

So they tugged the steak, riper than ever, away from him. O'Malley got a good firm bite on the skin of his neck. He stretched out and gripped the rim of the dumpster with his back feet (fortunately, the garbage bin was more than halfway full), and pulled and lifted for all he was worth. His father's body shifted some, but he was a pretty big cat, and a complete deadweight.

"I can't do it," gasped O'Malley. "It's too hard to pull him *up*."

The little green man said, "Try again." And as O'Malley did, the green man got a shoulder under the unconscious cat and *shoved* up as O'Malley *pulled* up, and their burden began to move—inch by inch they got him up the side and even had his head over the edge.

Then all of a sudden they heard the trash truck coming down the street. They were galvanized into even more frantic action—pulling, shoving, tugging at the limp body between them. Now the shoulders were over. Here came the truck, turning into the alley, its headlights sweeping the fence.

They could hardly breathe. Perspiration was in their eyes, and their muscles were aching. Still they struggled—now one leg was caught on the rim of the container—here came the truck—when suddenly enough of the old cat's weight was on the outside to pull his whole body over, and he fell with a soft "splump" to the ground in front of the dumpster.

"Hurry," gasped the little green man. "Pull him away." And they dragged the body away from the dumpster and around behind it next to the building.

Just in time! The truck came to a stop. Its metal arm reached out, grabbed the dumpster, hoisted it up, turned it over, then set it back down with a bang. The truck ground its gears and rumbled on down the alley to the back of the next store.

O'Malley and the little man sat there, dazed and exhausted, covered with smears of ill-smelling refuse better not thought about, O'Malley with a torn claw, and the little man with scratched and dirty hands.

"Oh my," said the little man. "Now we'd better see if that was all for nothing." And he bent to look at the unconscious cat lying at their feet in the dust of the alley. The object of his inspection looked very much as if it might truly have been "all for nothing." He looked and smelled worse than they did, and the bucket had not only knocked him out but given him a cut over one ear that was oozing blood.

After looking curiously at his father's face, O'Malley licked the wound to clean it up. As he did, the older cat's feet and the end of his tail began to twitch. O'Malley stepped back, and the little green man called to his charge, "Ginger, Ginger Filkins, are you all right?"

Ginger opened his eyes and said, "Of course I'm all right," and then looked around and asked, "What happened to my steak?" Then seeing O'Malley, "Who's this?"

"This is one of your sons, and your steak is in the trash truck down the street being squashed flat in its compactor. And that's just where *you'd* be if we hadn't pulled you out of the bin in the nick of time!" The little man was so irate that he sputtered. "I've warned you a hundred times about dumpsters, but do you listen?"

But he wound down a bit, and they all cleaned themselves up as best they could, and then started slowly back to Mrs. Scroggins'—all of them worn out and sleepy.

When they got there, the window was still open, and they stopped for a minute under it.

"Do you want to come in?" asked O'Malley. "Mrs. Scroggins will feed you in the morning, and I think she'd even take you in to live here if you want, especially when she sees that we get along."

The older cat looked at the soft window-seat and the empty milk dish and the last dying embers of the fire, and for a moment he seemed tempted. But then he shook himself and said, "No, I'm a roamer, and there's freedom in my Irish blood. The little man helps look out for me, and we make a good pair. The road is our home, at least for now. We'll sleep here under the window a while, and then go on. But thank you."

So O'Malley jumped up and through the window, and the little green man followed him. He fastened the latch again and then said, "I get weary now and then, but he always wants to see what's down the next street and around the corner. He's getting old though, and maybe one of these days we'll be back and accept your offer. At any rate, we thank you for your help." The little man walked through the window and dropped to the ground to lie down beside the now-sleeping ginger cat.

O'Malley washed himself a little more, then put his nose between his paws and slowly closed his eyes. When he opened them again, Mrs. Scroggins, in her old tattered bathrobe, was shaking up the fire and muttering to herself, "I wonder what that funny smell in here is."

When she opened the door for him to go out, O'Malley walked around the house and looked under the window, but there was no sign of his night visitors. He made sure to thoroughly clean his shining fur before he went back inside.

O'Malley is getting old now himself, though Mrs. Scroggins seems much as she has always been. And sometimes, especially on moonlit autumn nights when he is lying on the window-seat looking out at the bushes and walks rimed with early frost, he thinks of his father and the little green man. He wonders if they wander still, or whether some evening the little green man will walk through the window again and say, "We're back, come help me get your father in."

He dozes off, one ear always cocked for the sound of their return—an ageless little green man and an ancient Irish ginger cat.

Ann Gilson is a retired university librarian who has been active in animal rescue for more than sixty years. Her twin passions are books and cats, and she cares for a large collection of each.

DRAM, A RESCUE

by Lynn Calhoun

As told to Helen Hille

In the Beginning …

There were five. All were completely black, four identical longhairs: One, Two, Three, and Four. And one shorthair, Five. They couldn't see what color their mom was because their eyes were shut. The world was dark. A week later their eyes were open, and Mom had a face to go with the purr. Then Three grew up and spent lots of hours playing with his brothers and sister. They soon began to climb out of their box. They fought and played together, jumped on and chased each other around, and curled up together, and always there was Mom.

It turned out that all too soon it was time for the next adventure.

✳   ✳   ✳   ✳

Rescued …

Their person put the kittens in a box and taped it shut. After a brief car ride, the box was set down just outside the door to the liquor store in Sequim. It was a sunny morning, and inside the box the kittens were getting hot and thirsty. The clerk opening the store found the box. She called her friend who she knew rescued kittens. "Aaaah … help! What am I going to do with this box of kittens?" Her friend hopped in her car and came right over, and meanwhile the clerk took the box into the store where it was cooler. When the friend arrived, they opened the box and withdrew five little fur-balls, more tail than anything. The kittens were lethargic from the stifling heat, but the clerk and her friend gave them lots

- 49 -

of water and some kitten food from the store next door, and they quickly recovered.

*   *   *   *

Life #2

Well, cat people are cat people, and so the kittens went to their first foster home, a lovely place in the country. They had a double-decker cage for naptime and nighttime. They loved playing with the old cat, Trouble, but they didn't like the dogs much. The five took over the house. They were never shy, always rambunctious. Sister was petite compared to the rest of them. The other four were very big boys.

One night soon after they moved in, there was a very bad windstorm and a tree fell through the roof of the back bedroom where they slept. There were even branches in their cage, though none of the kittens were hurt. They couldn't stay there while the roof was being repaired, so their people called Safe Haven, and the cat rescue people found a new foster home for them.

*   *   *   *

Life #3

Their new foster family had socialized and fostered ever so many litters of kittens, and the kittens soon felt right at home. These people knew what a kitten likes. Proper litter boxes, cat trees, scratching posts, sunshine in a sun room, play time, lots of toys and an adoring set of foster parents. They had it all. FosterMom said it was time for them to have names. She wanted a touch of elegance, so she named them for liqueurs. There was White Russian (also known as Rushy), Ouzo, Drambuie, Kahlua and Tia Maria. Rushy had that "I'm in charge of this pack" look and he was definitely the leader.

At first they lived in a cage, and then after a very short while the kittens decided that kitty furniture and human furniture was more comfortable. So they began playing and sleeping on the couches and the little beds, and though the sunroom was theirs, they had the run of the whole house.

They had to wear different color collars so the KittyVet could tell them apart when it was time for their shots. Rushy's was multicolor, Ouzo's blue, Kahlua's purple, Tia Maria's pink. And Drambuie's was red.

When they were old enough for their little surgeries, they had them. No more little black kitties in the neighborhood … at least, none related to them.

They played with each other and with the toys. Then Kahlua invented this game where he'd run alongside of the human walking—okay, maybe in between the legs—and then stop, turn around, and look up to see exactly where the human was, and then dodge the feet. Once, though, the Man didn't play the game right. He fell down and hurt himself. Even though the Man thought of himself as clumsy and did not blame them, the kittens knew right away that this was Not a Very Good Game.

Shortly they would be heading into a new chapter in their lives.

✻ ✻ ✻ ✻

Life #4

Another family came over with a large beige carrier. It had a soft lion cushion in it. Dram went into the carrier to sniff it out, and Kahlua followed him in. The humans laughed and shut the door, and the kittens were off to another foster home. Dram and Kahlua never saw Ouzo or Tia Maria again, but they were getting big enough, and could handle that. The other three kittens went to a different foster home.

In Dram's and Kahlua's new foster home there were three Others. They were not happy to see the kittens. One ran away from home for a while but she came back. The new kittens were bigger than she was, and they were not yet six months old. She would "hisssss" at them, but they didn't go away. Dram taught Kahlua how to fetch the chenille ball when FosterMom would throw it down the hall. Kahlua taught Dram to drop it just out of reach so FosterMom would get some exercise too. They would play together and nap together. They were best buddies.

One day a lady came by to look at them. By then they were handsome and elegant boys. The lady took them home with her. She had to work during the daytime, and they got quite rambunctious when she wasn't there. Their game was Run the Mantel and Knock Things Off. The Lady did not like that game at all and brought them back to FosterMom. Oh well, it was just another camp-out.

Then one day Kahlua cut his paw and FosterMom took him to the KittyVet. The KittyVet thought the kittens (now *big* cats) had turned out just beautifully. She was the one who had done the surgeries when they were smaller. She knew of a man who had a need for Kahlua, and she called him, and soon Kahlua went to his new home. Without Kahlua, Dram was lonely. The foster home was nice enough but the three Others still didn't like having a kitten around. So Foster Mom decided it was time to bring Dram to Safe Haven so that he'd have a better chance to find His Forever Home.

So once again into the carrier. He got to take his favorite Lion cushion with him.

*   *   *   *

Life #5

At Safe Haven, he was taken downstairs to the big boys room. There were a few girl kitties in there too. No more kitten room for him, even though he had not yet seen his first birthday. One of the cats in the room seemed familiar to Dram. It was Rushy! What a handsome pair they were—the humans said so. By that night they were best buddies again. Then one day a lady came and wanted Rushy, and he left with her. It was only a few days after that when Dram's Forever Mom came to see him. She had come to choose a kitty for her birthday gift. There was just something special in her smile and voice, so Dram picked her. She only *thinks* she chose him. So he and his Lion cushion went home with her.

*   *   *   *

Life #6

Well, he and Mom got along famously. He taught her what Dram likes and what he doesn't like and she told him a few rules of the house. Unfortunately, she had a roommate who had different rules. So tearfully Mom called for some help, and Dram went back to Safe Haven while she found a new apartment of her own—with no roommate. It took a little while and Dram played with the guys there. Riley was his special buddy. Mom came to see him every day she could. Dram would sit by her feet, telling the world that he was Already Taken. She came to Safe Haven so often that after a while she learned to help take care of the cats there, and she became a volunteer.

Then one day she came in with Good News. "We have a new home in an apartment building downtown!" she told Dram. She put him into a carrier for a car ride to his new home.

*   *   *   *

Life #7

Dram: *I am now in my forever home! What a place this is! Mine, all mine! No Other to claim half my space. I am still training my true Mom. Every day she gets out the leash and we go on excursions. If the fire alarm goes off I head right for the carrier so Mom knows we have to be ready to evacuate. I've even taught her to bring my mouse back to me. Sometimes I bat it under the sofa or the refrigerator; she must bend and stretch, too, for her exercise. We cats know how important that stretching is. She gives me lots of toys, and food whenever I want it. And she plays with me. Having toys is nice but playing with me is nicer. Purr purr purr. I am so happy that I have my new Mom!*

*   *   *   *

And so they lived happily ever after.

Lynn Calhoun is a PFOA volunteer who lives in Port Angeles, Washington. She loves cats and is owned by a magnificent feline.

4 PAWS AWARD

Butch, the Canine Parish Assistant

by Ruth Gordon

At the age of 53, Father Patrick Downey Lannan, the beloved pastor of Nativity of Our Lord Catholic Church in St. Paul, Minnesota, began having heart problems. His doctors told him he must exercise more, but that wasn't something he liked to do. In fact, he found creative excuses to avoid any form of exercise. But one Saturday morning in May, Father called his friend Bill Beltz and asked him to drive him to the St. Paul Humane Society. Father Lannan had decided he needed a dog. It would be a mutually beneficial arrangement. He would be saving a dog from being destroyed. In return, the dog's need to be walked would provide him with company on his much needed exercise. A win-win situation.

Bill had known Father Lannan for many years, and was dubious. Father had never liked to walk and had never owned a dog. Bill urged him to think seriously and more realistically about the responsibilities of dog ownership—not just exercise, but feeding, grooming, veterinarian visits, training, etc. Reluctantly, Bill agreed to take him to the Humane Society, but he made Father promise not to be impulsive, to wait, to think about it a little longer and definitely not to come home with a dog right away. Father was pensive, but agreed.

When the two arrived at the shelter, they separated. Bill went through the facility fairly quickly, but Father Lannan walked among the hundred or more cages very thoughtfully, reading as much information as was available for each dog. He was especially interested in the reasons people gave for bringing a dog to the shelter. "Doesn't get along with our cat." "Not enough time to train."

"Moved." Father thought how sad it was that pets lost their homes because of such small problems, which could have been worked out.

After a long time, Father found Bill in the waiting room and said he had found a dog he liked very much. His name was Butch. He was a five-year-old small, mostly black lab with one blue eye and one brown eye. Father was quite enthusiastic, adding that the dog had been trained to work with the elderly. The dog's owner had moved to another state and for some reason could not or would not take Butch along.

Bill was wary, but Father arranged for the attendant to bring Butch to a small room where they could meet and interact with Butch directly and privately. It was obvious to Bill that Father Lannan had made up his mind, and Butch, looking quite scraggly from his shelter life, certainly seemed to have no doubts about going home with Father. Bill reminded Father of his promise. Father, a man of his word, had not forgotten, but he found a way to keep his promise in spite of his decision. The attendant said if Father would make a small down payment, they could hold the dog for twenty-four hours. He would get his money back if he changed his mind.

When Bill arrived at work on Monday, Father announced that he had bought the dog on Sunday. However, Butch needed to have a veterinarian check him before he could be released. By Monday afternoon, a very scruffy looking Butch arrived at his new home, the Nativity Church Rectory where Father lived in a second floor apartment. Father liked to say that he quickly got Butch "fluffed and buffed" so he looked his best when he began meeting his new family.

From the beginning it was obvious that this was going to be a special relationship. Father Lannan felt needed in a whole new way, and Butch adored Father and stayed at his side wherever he went. Butch soon became a full participant in the life of the church. He was a special friend of the school children, and took to greeting parishioners on Sundays. And yes, Father Lannan finally got some exercise from walking his enthusiastic new friend.

Whenever Father came home from a meeting, the first thing he asked was, "Where's Butch?" and "How's my Butch?" And when Butch heard him, he'd come bounding up, wiggling his whole body with joy, wagging his tail vigorously, and making wonderful eye contact with both his blue eye and his brown eye. Father said Butch was a true gift from heaven. Butch obviously felt the same.

Father Lannan regularly visited Our Lady of Good Counsel Hospice, a home for terminally ill cancer patients run by the Dominican Sisters of Hawthorne, Servants of Relief for Incurable Cancer.

On one of Father's visits to the hospice, he took Butch with him. Butch seemed to know just what to do. Following the Activities Director, Carla Stafford, as she visited patients, he nuzzled outstretched hands in his loving way, warming hearts and lifting spirits up and down the halls.

After several such visits, Butch was given a permanent part-time job. Every Tuesday morning, Carla stopped at the rectory and took him to work with her. Someone else, often Bill, would bring him back in the late afternoon. Butch worked six to eight hours at the cancer home on Tuesdays for almost three years.

His routine was always the same. He stayed with Carla wherever she went. When she would let a side rail down, Butch's nose went immediately to the patient's hand. If she patted the bed, he put both feet up on the bed. Some patients asked that his warm body lie beside them on the bed for a while. Butch, Carla, and all the patients looked forward to Tuesdays.

At the rectory, the sight of Butch at Father Lannan's side was an integral part of the landscape. On their walks, Butch always matched his pace to Father's.

Father bought 25 bandannas for Butch. Green for St. Patrick's Day; red, white and blue for the 4th of July and so on. He saw to it that Butch wore the appropriate bandanna on both religious and national holidays.

At Christmas time, the parish always erected a Nativity scene outside the church. One year a parishioner found a large black ceramic Labrador retriever at a craft store and bought it in honor of Butch. Eventually, the ceramic Butch, touched up to have one blue eye and one brown, and wearing Butch's tags and red bandanna, was placed in the crèche. There it was alongside the shepherds, the three Wise Men, Mary, Joseph, and the infant Jesus. When Father Lannan saw it, he thought it was truly funny and not inappropriate. Most parishioners loved having Butch in their crèche. Father's advice to anyone who didn't, was to "go home, have a martini and let your hair down."

Seeing Butch in the crèche prompted the children to ask if Jesus had a dog. Father answered honestly. He said, "Yes, Jesus could have had a dog." The children were satisfied.

The area Archbishop also owned a dog, a golden retriever named Megan. When Butch had his story written up in the *St. Paul Pioneer Press* as well as the local neighborhood paper, the Archbishop called Father Lannan to complain that *his* dog had never been written up in the newspaper. It is said that Father Lannan answered, "What has your dog ever done for a parish?"

Father Lannan particularly enjoyed leading pilgrimages to the Holy Land with some of the parishioners. Late in 1998 Father Lannan led his fifth pilgrimage to the Holy Land. About a week into the trip, the church received the shocking news that Father Lannan had died in Israel. While everyone knew that he was in poor health, they were nevertheless stunned.

As his grieving family and congregation prepared for the return of Father Lannan's body, there were discussions about the fate of Butch. It was decided that Butch should not stay at the rectory without Father Lannan. Several parishioners offered to take him, but Father's family felt that Bill would be the logical person because he and Butch knew each other so well. Bill and his wife, Kathy, a teacher at the Nativity School, discussed the matter with all the pros and cons. Everyone agreed that their home would be the right place for Butch, but not until after Father Lannan's burial.

Father Lannan's wake was a solemn affair. He had so many friends among the clergy, among the congregation, and among a wide variety of community groups, that the collective grief seemed almost unbearable. Butch was allowed to visit the casket. He sniffed around it both thoroughly and with curiosity. When he left the room, Butch went out into the rose garden and did something he had never done before. He sat down and howled without stopping for several hours.

On the day of the funeral, Butch followed the casket down the long aisle in the processional. He lay quietly beside the casket during the service. After the recessional, Butch was taken to the rectory where he stayed during the burial. He had said his "good-bye."

When Bill and Kathy returned from the cemetery, they took Butch to their home, his new home. When he first entered their house, he seemed a bit anxious. Then he sat down and fixed his blue eye and his brown eye on an unadorned wall in their living room. They watched him stare at the wall for several minutes. Finally, he turned around and faced them, relaxed and settled in. This curious behavior certainly raised questions. Some speculated that Father Lannan was there to tell Butch that everything would be all right and this would be where he was to live now.

Butch has had a very good life with Bill and Kathy. People often stop them on the street because they've heard about him. Members of his church community and the Nativity School children are especially glad to see the beloved dog of their beloved Father Lannan.

He has been loved by many and continues to be loved. He remains a very loving dog. His ceramic statue sits outside the entry to Bill and Kathy's house. They change bandannas on the statue according to the season or holiday, just as Father Lannan used to do with Butch.

Ruth Gordon is a life-long resident of St. Paul, Minnesota. She has had a distinguished career in nursing, is associate professor emerita from the University of Minnesota, and author of many textbooks. When her beloved golden retriever, Ben, died, she turned to writing true dog stories. It Takes a Dog to Raise a Village *and* Good Dogs, *both published by Willow Creek Press, were written in her retirement.*

© Raven 2007

JOHN & SHADOW

Raven O'Keefe

4 PAWS AWARD

My Mother's Freckles

by DeeAnn Nelson

Saturdays,
when the sun slants late through the panes
of the long front windows,
my mother
slips from her chair
into the carpet
   on elbow
to flutter the dozing cat's
plumpchested fur.
Soon, she too, is stretched
full length, in the square of sun
   speaking quietly
matter-of-factly
to the slowblinking cat
   her freckled arms rosy orange in the sunlight
her book tossed gently aside,
pages floating above the heavy yarn
of the carpeting.
In a moment she too is asleep.

DeeAnn Nelson lives in Port Townsend, Washington, with her PFOA-adopted cat Sunnie, and previously appeared as Miss March in PFOA's first calendar in 2004.

SUZIE

by Terry Kush

I did not want a dog. I was not ready. I was still grieving our boy, Henry, our ever so handsome yellow lab we had buried way too recently.

I did not want a dog. I had no time. I had to finish my thesis and could tolerate no distractions.

I did not want a dog.

Then I walked into the house after a shopping trip, and my husband called out, "Honey, come see what I have." There, in the palm of one hand, was a teeny tiny black puppy. The animal shelter had sponsored a pet adoption at the local pet store down the street, and she was the very last remaining puppy. I think she was waiting for him. Anyway, they told him that she was a mixed breed, SharPei and Labrador Retriever. She did have the wrinkles and looked kind of like a lab, but not quite.

She told me her name was Suzie, and she joined our family with the cats, chickens, rabbits, ducks, and geese. I carried Suzie all around the house, she was just so little. She would nap in her wooden orange crate and whimper when she woke up. I would run into "her room" mumbling baby talk about what a nice nap she had taken and how it was time to go outside and potty. Really, I don't recall being that attentive to my daughters when they were babies!

Somehow I finally did finish my thesis, and Suzie grew bigger and taller and heavier. She grew into a really big girl! She topped out at about a hundred pounds and grew so tall that I no longer needed to bend down to pet her. Forget trying to pick her up or carry her. The shelter people forgot to mention the Great Dane and Doberman breeds in her family heritage, but her appearance certainly confirmed those influences.

Suzie is a gentle girl and a very old spirit. She understands our language and can tell time, even without looking at a clock! I have always felt that she was much smarter than most people and could have better performed their tasks if only she could drive a car or type on a computer.

Suzie has lived with us now for fifteen years. She has gotten gray, and so have we; she has arthritis and has a hard time getting up or getting down, and so do we. I guess we are growing old together. Suzie is our good friend and companion. To this day I will never understand why my husband stopped at that pet store at that particular day and time, but I am sure glad he did.

Terry Kush was born in Los Angeles where she lived until she retired from telecommunications management. After retirement she moved to beautiful Port Angeles where she lives with her wonderful husband and a very spoiled tabby cat.

METAPHOR MOUSE

by Michael Marcus

I was to spend the first half of my vacation painting the bathroom and porches, the second with the four grandchildren who managed, conveniently, to have birthdays in the same week of August. Instead, I flew to southern California. My mother was in the hospital again. She was over 93 years old and had been hospitalized several times in the last few years, but this was somehow different. Her difficulty swallowing had progressed, and it was clear she'd ruled out a feeding tube. She was down to about seventy pounds, and fading much more rapidly than the family had expected.

My kids had been visiting her often, sometimes with their kids. They accepted the "no heroic measures" directive in theory, but were less comfortable with it than my sister and I, who had attended Dad's last illness when my kids were teenagers.

The cab driver had no trouble finding Verdugo Hills Hospital from the Burbank Airport. I got the impression the path was well worn. My niece Nancy had hired an attendant for my mother, and it was Annie I first met in the room in TCU on the top floor. I wondered whether the "T" was for "terminal" before learning this was the "*transitional* care unit." Mother's neighbors indeed seemed to leave in both directions.

Mother brightened when I walked in, noticed my new hearing aids immediately, and pronounced them "inevitable" before falling back into sleep. My daughter Andréa arrived a bit later with her family, and Mother woke long enough to appreciate the presence of the two-year-old twins. Later Andréa drove me and my suitcase to my son Jacobus's house, in the Honda she'd acquired from Mother after Mother finally relinquished her keys, having first beaten the California DMV into submission for having the temerity to take away her license for doing 30 on a freeway. That half-hour drive around the northern edge of the San Fernando Valley to Santa Clarita was a route with which I would become very familiar in the next two weeks.

At my son's house, Andréa and her husband Geoff had prepared a simple meal, which was a great comfort, as they share my vegetarianism. After dinner I was sitting in a daze, treasuring a low ebb in my thoughts of Mother and death. "I hate to do this to you," Andréa began, "but there's an injured baby rat in the yard."

All of us—Mother, my kids, their spouses, my wife—easily qualify as animal lovers. Both kids have dogs and cats; Sharon and I have Newfoundland dogs (we had a cat who lived to sixteen, but Sharon is allergic so I'm forbidden to adopt another). We all assume that upon encountering an injured or unfortunate animal, we have some responsibility to respond. But "baby rat" revealed another strain altogether, as this was no baby rat but a full-grown tiny field mouse.

Rodents have somehow acquired the enmity of much of mankind. I suppose spreading the Black Plague and competing with starving people for the earth's grain yield gives the dominant faction all the argument they need. But "baby rat" turned out to be the misinformation by which to repel any empathy for mice. Understand that Andréa is quite knowledgeable about wildlife, having volunteered for months at a marine mammal rescue operation. That she thought this otherwise pitiable creature a baby "rat" evidences the phobic strength of the disfavor heaped upon rodents—Micky, Minnie and Mighty Mouse notwithstanding.

I easily scooped up the mouse in an empty quart yogurt container. She—gender distinction is easy in mature mice and rats even with a top view, for reasons having to do with their prolificacy—was clearly in very great trouble. Hunkered down and shivering, she was overrun with tiny ants. She had no strength with which to evade me; I doubted she even noticed my intervention. I was well aware that she might be carrying all sorts of disease; even I had no intention of contracting bubonic plague and carrying it into Verdugo Hills Hospital. Though I wanted to know if she had any obvious injuries, I made no effort to examine her. I thought her main enemy was shock if she were not already dying of internal bleeding or poisoning. My guess was that she had been assaulted by one of the household cats, but spared (or deprived of) a quicker death by automatic sprinklers. She was, after all, wet.

I learned that the tiny ants are Argentinean in origin and particularly industrious in disaggregating any living thing that might provide sustenance for the good of the order. I had no wish to harm the ants, but determined that they had jumped the gun with this creature and had to leave her alone at least for now. I noticed that many of the ants had departed the mouse for the walls of the yogurt container. By gently transferring the mouse to another container, I was able to shake off any that stayed behind, wait for more to take to the walls of the new container, and repeat the process until I had separated the mouse from all but a dozen ants. These I lured one at a time onto the head of the plunger of a tiny syringe. The syringe was for Uki, the diabetic Samoyed who came with Geoff, Andréa and the twins to visit Beau the Shepherd, Jack the Jack Russell, and various cats who live with Jacobus and Hazell. The mouse wouldn't or couldn't take milk from the syringe, but the syringe plunger worked very well to remove the remaining ants.

I sat for a long time watching this pathetic little being. From time to time, her shaking would become so severe that she would vibrate furiously as if she were suffering electrocution by household current.

I remembered having seen a hamster cage in Jacobus's house on a previous visit, so I described it to Andréa, who immediately retrieved it from its perch on a counter in the master bath. (By cell phone conversation with Hazell the next day, I learned that the cage was kept at the ready precisely to rescue critters injured by the cats.) I tore up some newspaper for nesting material (had I looked in the master bath, I would have found more suitable commercial hamster shavings), filled the water bottle, put some peanut butter and nuts in a dish, and placed the yogurt container on its side in the hamster cage. I believed this was the best I could do. I knew from a prior rescue attempt with a Portland opossum that veterinarians would have no part in my folly, and that my best hope for outside help with this project would probably lead to a hungry (or indifferent) snake. So I put the hamster cage in the room I was using, and turned out the lights. I was sure this was futile but I couldn't bring myself to put this creature "out of its misery." I vaguely recalled some fifty years earlier my father explaining that kindness forced him to use a shovel to behead a squirrel run over by a car but still thrashing. I expected that at best we could provide warmth, comfort, and whatever companionship could be appreciated at some level until "nature took its course."

Before I left for the hospital the next morning, I noticed that the mouse had obviously made the rounds of the cage and consumed some of the food I'd left for her. She was hunched on the floor of the cage, with no sign of tremors; eyes wide open, beady and bright; whiskers twitching inquisitively. I was encouraged, but hardly confident of her recovery. I made sure she had food and water, and left for Verdugo Hills. Andréa and I agreed the mouse seemed more likely to make it than Mother.

It was surreal to be sitting with a parent for hours contemplating her death and her life. Time would not have its usual meaning. Mother and I had long ago acknowledged our difficulty in spending extended time together, but over those long days we had some wonderful conversations. Gone was all artifice. She had energy for few words, and her circumstances stripped all pretense and device from our communication. She apologized for her parenting; I protested that she had given me life and taught me compassion. (I didn't tell her about the mouse, though. Her own rodent phobia was compounded by frightening hours spent as a child visiting an elderly relative in an institution she recalled primarily for its prominent rats. Were they, too, mice?) She was comforted by confirmation of the health of the marriages she assessed: mine and those of my children. She allowed me to massage her feet—a degree of intimacy we had never shared as mother and son. She enjoyed the photos I displayed on my small laptop: the flowers I captured when I crossed the street for lunch, the photos of the "greats" as she called her prized great-grandchildren, and photos of the exploits of our newest Newfoundland, Sonnet. All of this was experienced in the lucid gaps among spells of sleep and the recurring therapies, changes, blood draws and IV adjustments. I held her hand much of the time she slept, noticing on my wrist on this the 17th anniversary of Father's death the watch she had transferred from him to me as he lay dying—noticing also that this was the first of these anniversaries *she* appeared not to notice.

The IV nourishment had been started days before I arrived. The doctor recommended it because Mother was not able to take nourishment by mouth and the family repeatedly reported "no feeding tube" as Mother's instructions. The Monday after I arrived, through great effort employing aides and volunteers, Mother was taken to X-ray for a swallowing study. We had all had the impression that her progressive difficulty was neurological. The swallowing study, however, showed that the problem resided in her lower esophagus. Although her airway closed too slowly to avoid aspiration with thin liquids, she could swallow sufficiently viscous mixtures. But because she had lost motility in her lower esophagus, whatever she swallowed backed up without passing to her stomach, and she quite naturally responded by choosing not to continue swallowing. We learned there were medications that might fix this and planned to discuss it with the doctor, who would surely prescribe one when he received the speech therapist's report.

When I returned from the hospital that day, my daughter-in-law Hazell and I conferred on the mouse. We agreed that it seemed recovered and that releasing her the next day was probably best. *Where* to release her was a dilemma, however.

Lush lawns, the nourishing excesses of suburban living, and water itself were convenient to rodents among houses in their gated community. But there were also numerous assorted neighborhood pets to deal with, including Jacobus's and Hazell's five cats and two dogs. Releasing the mouse nearby would invite a repetition of her plight—or worse. The alternative was to take her across the freeway and into some nearby hills, which were typified by decomposed granite, and tenacious brush that didn't seem to need much water. Here, of course, she would take her chances among the hordes of other prey and their predators—most visibly, coyotes, but also snakes and birds of prey.

I chose the more natural path for whatever remained of her life, and prepared food and liquid to leave with her in hopes of increasing her chances. I hiked some distance into the brush, ignoring the scratches and scrapes inflicted by the protective aspects of the vegetation, and carefully laid out the provisions. I opened the cage. The mouse quickly moved to the open platform that had been the door, stared straight at me for a few seconds, then darted away and out of sight faster than my eye could follow. That was a great sign: all of her reflexes and instincts were apparently functioning, and she probably had the same odds of survival as any of her ilk. I knew thought was behind that last stare, but I had no clue what she was thinking. Gratitude would be too anthropomorphic a projection; bewilderment plausible; calculation for escape likely.

Back at the hospital, we had to intercept well-meant juice cartons with protruding straws, delivered by volunteers who didn't notice the "NPO" scrawled on a note above Mother's bed, and probably didn't understand that NPO meant "nothing by mouth." The doctor was skeptical about medication to improve esophageal function, but would give it a try. The speech therapist, however, was certain that Mother could gain some nourishment by eating properly thickened liquids slowly, but we would need to give the process time to work, with hopes that the new medication would allow this source of nutrition to prove adequate.

During the sunset drive back to Jacobus's, I realized a rare but light rain had fallen, and immediately thought that the moisture might increase the chances that the mouse would make it.

Near the end of the week, it appeared that feeding by tiny spoonfuls was not going to provide adequate nutrition for Mother. The doctor was impatient, and felt we should stop the IV feeding, transfer Mother to hospice and "let her go." If she didn't want a feeding tube, we were somehow cheating by feeding her through an IV. He stopped in once when she was coughing, and pronounced this a "vicious circle"—that she was aspirating whenever she tried to eat. I was certain that this was an artifact of his timing: he knew we were trying to feed her, found her coughing when he stopped in for his 120 second visit, and assumed the two were related. The respiratory therapist, however, repeatedly declared her lungs clear, and from our perspective and the speech therapist's the coughing was unrelated to her feeding schedule. But it didn't matter. She was not getting enough by mouth to survive, and all agreed that the IV was "temporary."

So it was time to make a decision. My sister Jane and I talked, and I later talked to Andréa. When I explained all of the considerations as I understood them, Andréa shook some sense into me: "Has anyone asked *her*?" This reeled in my thoughts a while, and I retraced. We were all operating under the assumption of an instruction to the effect of "no heroic measures." Jane had seen Mother react to the sight of feeding tube patients, and heard her declare that she never wanted to be on a feeding tube. The combination yielded the current family position, but we needed to be careful here: you don't starve someone to death without being damn sure of what you're doing.

What Andréa's question resurrected was that the "durable power of attorney for health care" Mother had executed did not give anyone the right to make decisions for her as long as she had the ability to make those decisions for herself. Even beyond the issue of whether IV feeding or a stomach tube, for that matter, represented a "heroic measure," and whether any resulting prognosis was one of "reasonable" recovery, Mother had the right to decide all of this for herself if she were able, and she was predictably awake and lucid every day. Regardless of what she thought (or knew) of stomach tubes before her life depended on one, she had the right to make her own decisions now.

I now knew what I had to do. I spent a couple of hours composing a presentation, "We Need to Know Your Wishes," on my laptop that laid out the various conditions from which Mother suffered, the choices facing her, and the consequences of each choice. I set out the nature and prognosis of her COPD, what we had learned about her swallowing problem, that medication was not sufficient to allow her to take sufficient nutrition by mouth, and that the IV feeding could not continue indefinitely, and why. I explained how feeding tubes work (they do not enter the stomach through the throat, but by way of a stoma created surgically in the abdomen; they can be detached and do not interfere with breathing, speaking, or movement). I explained that her choices were: that continuing the IV would lead to kidney failure or infection; that detaching the IV without a stomach tube would lead to starvation; and that with a stomach tube she had a good chance of regaining strength, mobility and more time to enjoy her "greats."

I had to leave for Santa Barbara for the twins' birthday party over the weekend, so I looked for ways to print out the presentation for Jane to share with

Mother as soon as she could process the information. Cable compatibility was a problem, but a helpful hospital librarian allowed me to type out the presentation on a computer and print it out. It was seven pages long, with large type, and in landscape format. I left it with Jane and drove to Santa Barbara, staying in touch by cell phone.

By the end of the day, Mother had studied the pages and chosen a stomach tube. It would be inserted first thing next week.

The twins' party was a great success. Andréa had baked a suitably wholesome birthday cake, and swarms of kids and their parents soon overran the house and yard. Andréa and Sharon had purchased a piñata, and noisemakers and child-hood-development-friendly treats with which to fill it. I was in charge of stuffing the piñata and hanging it, and objected that it was inappropriate to have these kids beat what looked like a pony into smithereens to reach candy. Sharon (emphatically) and Andréa (less so) defended the choice because this paper pony stood on rails that made it look like a rocking horse, not a "real" horse. I stated for the record that I was not persuaded, but went about my work. When its time came, each of the little ones did his or her very best to destroy the white pony with pink trim. One of the fathers muttered something about "Lord of the Flies." Andréa confessed the error, and resolved that next year's piñata wouldn't resemble a living creature.

The next day, I drove back to Verdugo Hills and spent the rest of my time with Mother. She had already gained a great deal of weight, though much was evidenced by edema (which would resolve over time). I showed her the many photos of the twins and their birthday party, which delighted her. When we got to the piñata, she frowned and pointed in disapproval. I was able to relieve her concern by assuring her that never again would her "greats" be offered a piñata that looked like an animal.

Weeks later, Mother was able to move out of Verdugo Hills and into a nursing home, a step up in level of care from the retirement home she'd left for the hospital. I was getting encouraging reports from Jacobus and Andréa and more cautious reports from Jane, who saw Mother when her mood wasn't elevated by great-grandchildren. She was comfortable, and enjoying the letters and photos I sent her recounting her grand-dog Sonnet's exploits. But she couldn't read more than a page at a time without exhaustion.

I got to see her one more time as I was passing through on the way home from a diving trip with Jacobus. She was hospitalized again with pneumonia, but was out of immediate danger, comfortable, and sleeping a great deal. She seemed to be enjoying her dreams, and was almost immediately lucid upon awakening for a minute or so. She was happy to see me, smiled, repeated some life-summing reflections, and fell back to sleep. We realized that her life was coming to an end, but that it could be weeks or months before "things changed."

I was relieved to find that the fires that were raging through southern California at the time had spared the region of Mother's hospital, my children's houses, and the hills in which I had released the mouse. I wondered if she were still alive, whether she was in immediate danger.

One day I awoke at around four AM with a strange form of heartburn. I remember thinking I'd not experienced this before. I took an antacid, went back to sleep, and got on the Nordic Track at the usual time, come morning. I was interrupted by a telephone call from my sister: Mother had been discovered, dead, in her bed by the early shift at her nursing home.

In life we interact with so many beings, on so many levels. Parents and children, extended family, adversaries and friends, coworkers and subjects of our careers—even strangers across the globe whose acts or choices affect the food we eat, the price of our fuel, our elections, debates, fears, jokes, and taxes—and whose lives our events often profoundly change. As with laws of physics, each encounter produces some effect on every person or being involved. Our perceptions of our impact on each other are enormously diverse. We accuse the insect of flying into our windshield when we drive at a hundred times its speed; we are bewildered by the hatred of those we purport to "liberate" by killing their loved ones with "smart bombs," and of those whose family homes are demolished by our cherished allies. We nurture companion animals, slaughter lambs, calves, and adult food animals in "kill plants" known to the public by gentler names; we hunt and kill wildlife for sport. Of the inevitable impact of each meeting of beings, some are predictable, like children modeling their parents; some reflect chaos—pigpen design in China spawns a flu that kills elders in Chicago; others evince uncertainty that somehow selects which of us will be taken by our self-inflicted predators: autos, addictions, and the industrial chemicals that bring us cancers.

So I have no clue whether my interaction with my mother and her choice of a stomach tube, or with the mouse and her destiny, was for better or worse, inevitable or accidental, noble or pathetic, or just noise in our dimension.

But I do know something of death, if only from the myopia of my own perspective.

Michael Marcus has been an Oregon trial judge since 1990, a vegetarian since 1975, for many years a supporter of his local Newfoundland dog club, www.crnewf-

club.com, *and long a proponent of intelligent criminal sentencing reform,* www.smartsentencing.com. *He, his wife, Sharon, and their two Newfoundlands, Sonnet and Petra, live in Portland, Oregon.*

4 PAWS AWARD
Historical Critters

BILLY

by Elizabeth Fletcher Barlow

In 1896, when my father was eleven, he came with his parents and family to a homestead on the Lower Hoh River on the Olympic Peninsula. He took up a homestead of his own on the north side of the Hoh in 1906, when he turned twenty-one. He made his living with packhorses—a weekly mail contract to Forks, and bringing needed items to people between the Lower Hoh and Forks. He also packed for surveyors, oil explorers and others who needed things moved throughout the area. There were only trails, no roads, in those days.

I remember the names of most of Dad's horses: Buckskin … Dobbin … Peggy … Dan. Selim and Topsy were purchased from what was left from the Ruby Beach Gold Mine, a fraudulent stock selling scheme in the mid-1920s. My dad had his favorite riding horses, as well as packhorses he could trust with specific loads—dynamite, cases of gasoline and such.

Dad acquired Billy from his brother-in-law, our nearest neighbor. Billy was a sorrel (reddish) colored horse with a white blaze on his face. At that time horse trading was the equivalent of selling or trading used cars today. You were not always told of the little eccentricities that came with the deal.

Billy had a special talent. Our rain-forest climate meant the trails were extremely muddy for a good part of the year. Settlers worked on improving them in lieu of paying taxes. Great improvements were made by laying cedar puncheon (split planks of random widths) in the boggy areas. But before that planking was put in, a pole was often laid alongside a treacherous area so foot travelers wouldn't have to slog through a mire. There were also foot logs spanning creek gullies before bridges were built. Well, Billy must have felt the same way as people did about mud, because with all the boldness and balance of a tightrope artist, he would walk those poles and even foot logs. My dad sometimes arranged to have riders transported by Billy—to his amusement (I don't know about theirs!).

Elizabeth Fletcher Barlow grew up and has lived on the Hoh River nearly all of her life. She is the granddaughter of John "the Iron Man of the Hoh" and Dora Huelsdonk. She is a professional artist and has a degree in botany from the University of Washington. She has had a lifelong interest in animals, big and small.

DAD AND BILLY

Submitted by Elizabeth Fletcher Barlow

4 PAWS AWARD
Best Fiction

MIDNIGHT SNOW IN TIME

by Ann Gilson

It was almost midnight when old Mrs. Olson woke up slowly. Instead of the darkness she expected, her room was filled with a dim, pearly light, and puzzled, she lay listening quietly for a moment after opening her eyes.

The sound of the town clock slowly striking twelve a couple of miles away resonated faintly in the silence. She thought, sleepily, "Why, it's the magic wishing hour," and then she remembered, "Oh my, and today's my birthday again—I'm seventy."

She woke up then—she was sure she did—and looked out the little window beside her bed. Mrs. Olson's bed was the old fashioned kind, built into the wall of her sitting room, with cupboards underneath, a curtain that could be pulled to close it off, and a little window with four tiny panes that could be opened to the garden outside.

She opened the window now and peered out. The source of the peculiar light in the room was very evident when she did—the whole world was covered with almost a foot of light fluffy snow.

It covered every tree and bush, every pot and rock, the top of the old fence around the garden, and the wooden steps under the window where the cats often sat to watch the garden doings and soak up the sun. The whole sky had a cloudy white cover and light reflected from it to the snow then back again. This pearly luminescence showed the outside world almost as clearly to Mrs. Olson as the sun of daytime would have.

"How pretty everything is," she thought and pulled herself up and settled the pillow more comfortably against the headboard, the better to enjoy the unusual scene.

What happened next was so peculiar that Mrs. Olson wondered if she might be dreaming. A little hillock of snow mounded over what she assumed was a shrub, moved slightly, roiled a couple of seconds, and then seemed to collapse as a small snowperson stood up.

He was only the size of a child, with fair skin and silvery, shimmering eyes and hair. His clothes seemed somehow insubstantial, no color and yet all colors, with the texture of new fallen snow and something of that color, though it was hard to tell exactly where they began and ended.

"My goodness! Where did you come from?" gasped Mrs. Olson, rather stupidly, she later thought.

"I've always been here," replied the little creature in a soft and sweetly silver voice. "Don't you remember me?"

"Remember you? I don't *think* I do," the old woman said. And she closed her eyes to search back in her memory. Slowly, slowly she went—ten years, twenty years, thirty years. Finally, more than sixty years back, she found him, and her eyes popped open.

"My goodness," she said, and the small girl who lived inside her still, after all those years, slipped out the window and joined him in the snow.

"My goodness," she repeated, taking his hand. "I'd completely forgotten you, Kedrick. How could that have happened?"

Kedrick's eyes were very old in his young face when he smiled at her. "I've been right here, Mary, where I always am, in the snow world. It's just that our worlds haven't been in phase for a long time now, and we couldn't meet. So I dropped into your forgetfulness."

Mary looked about her. Yes, it was still her garden she stood in. There was the Cornish Gilliflower apple tree she'd planted forty years ago, and there the Celsiana rose she'd tended for thirty years, both transformed under the magic of the snow.

Yet it *wasn't* her garden, quite, either. For as she stood there, eight years old again and only slightly taller than Kedrick, perfectly warm in the icy world around her, other small hillocks of snow rose from the landscape, crumpled, and she was soon surrounded by a whole band of merry snowpersons.

A couple of them pulled small dry branches from bundles on their backs, and others smoothed the snow under the old apple tree. They built a small, bright fire there, and soon all were sitting around it on the snow. Silver goblets of clear sweet liquor were passed from hand to hand, and a big basket of little crisp cakes also moved about.

There were calls, finally, "Callea, a song," and a pretty snowgirl started to sing. Her voice, with almost heartbreaking sweetness, led the company in airs while the fire flickered on their faces in the snowlight.

As the last song died away, Mary looked about her, then back at Kedrick, and asked slowly, "Why are you here tonight?"

So Kedrick told his tale. "When our world and yours were last in phase, when it was last possible for you to step into ours and you to be with us, and when we could last step into your garden (which is also ours in our world), Callea's sister, Maylee, was with us. But when the sun rose and our worlds separated, we discovered she was no longer among us.

"We believe," he continued, "that she stayed behind until it was too late because she could not bear to leave your cat Razmus, and she was trapped in your world. We've come to find her and take her home, and we need your help, and Raz's."

"Oh dear," said Mary, dismay on her face and in her sinking heart. "But don't you know? In this mortal world our cats do not live as long as we do. It's a great grief to us who love them. Razmus has been dead for more than fifty years, and I haven't seen Maylee since that night you all were here. It's been more than sixty years." She paused with tears in her eyes. "Whatever shall we do?"

Kedrick did not reply, and seemed to be thinking deeply. The others sat silent. Finally he said, "That's strange, because I thought I saw Razmus sleeping on one of your pillows just before you slipped out the window and joined us."

"Oh, no," said Mary. "That was Rachel—she's actually just a kitten yet. A neighbor needed a home for her, and she came to live with me and the other cats a couple of months ago." She thought a moment and then said, "You know, she does look almost exactly like Raz did, so I can see why you mistook her for him."

Her brow furrowed as she thought some more, and finally she said, very hesitantly, "It's rather odd, but now that I think of it, it seems as if I've always had one cat among my clowder that has looked somewhat like Razzie. Black and white, sometimes long-haired, sometimes short, a black spot on or near her nose, a white blaze on his back—and always into things, mostly trouble. After Razmus died, Gypsy came, and after him, Paddington. Paddington lived nearly twenty years, and after him was Grubby, and a year after Grubby left us, McGillicuddy came for fourteen years. He died last winter and six months later Rachel was born to the neighbor's cat, and now she's mine."

Mary looked up. "You know, I never noticed that, in all these years, with so many cats coming and living their lives with me, and going on at last. Do you suppose it means anything? I never noticed the whole line, though I've come to believe that there's a connection between Razzie and Rachel. They're so alike."

Kedrick's face lit up while she spoke, and the others had listened intently. "We'll see," he said, and stepped up to the window and called softly, "Rachel. Rachel, come on out."

Mary's eyes followed his gaze. There sat Rachel in the window, surveying them all, the firelight striking sparks in her blue-gold eyes, so like Razzie's golden ones.

"I wondered when you would think of me," said Rachel in her soft, throaty kitten voice, and she moved from the window, down the steps and walked over to join them at the fire. In the snowshine, her beautiful black and white body, with its tiny Manx suggestion of a tail, seemed to glow with vitality.

"Why, whatever do you mean, Rachel?" asked Mary. And, "Can you help us?" asked Kedrick.

"I think so. I hope so," replied Rachel. "It has been a long, long time that we have carried the knowledge that you want, and we have despaired many times. Maylee said you'd be back and that we must be here when you came. But I must say we'd begun to doubt her. It's been hard to keep the memory through so many lives. You see, I'm part of the same consciousness as Razmus and all the others, taking many mortal forms. But usually we don't carry memories from life to life, and that has been the hard part. When Raz loved Maylee and she stayed behind with him, he knew you'd be back for her and that she would return to her own world. But when he died no one would know where she was, so he had to, somehow, be here when you came."

"But, how?" asked Mary.

"Well, you always took in lots of cats," said Rachel, "and made a home for them. But you always saw to it that your cats had no kittens, so I couldn't be born into this household. So I had to arrange to be reborn into this world somewhere near you, and then find my way to you.

"Sometimes I didn't make it, and died under the wheels of a car or as a meal for some other creature. But I'd try again, and always finally found you, and you'd take me in. Then I'd wait, and finally my life would end, and then I'd do it all over again. I'm glad you've finally come, Kedrick," she ended simply.

"I'm glad, too, Rachel," said Kedrick. "And now you can tell us what you've spent so many lifetimes remembering. Where is Maylee?"

"You remember how special Maylee was. You called her 'the changing one' because unlike all the other snowpeople, who are eternally the same, she changed and grew continuously. Her heart was full of love for everything in the universe, for all the beings in all the worlds. That's why she loved me as Razzie and why she was able to leave the snow world. In a way, she always became a part of everything she loved.

"And when she stayed with Raz, she could no longer be a snowperson, not in this world. It would not be safe for her, she could not exist here. So she changed once more, into the one person in this world who also loved Razzie, and whom he loved—Mary."

"Mary! You mean *me?*" cried Mary. "But I'm not Maylee."

Kedrick and the others looked amazed and uncertain.

"Aren't you?" asked Rachel. "Aren't you 'the changing one'? Could old Mrs. Olson be sitting here with us? I think," she went on, "though I'm not sure, that you as Mary and you as Maylee were born, two halves of the same being, into two different worlds long ago. And I think it's been Razzie's task, and all the others, and mine, to bring you together as one whole, through our love for you."

And Mary shut her eyes and looked into her heart, and found Maylee waiting there for her, and she was whole at last.

"Will you come with us?" asked Kedrick.

Then Mary Maylee put her hand in his and her arm around Rachel. As the fire died out they all gathered around a slowly rising hummock of snow. Then it parted, and they walked inside and on into an ever-new world of snow and beauty and joy and love.

*   *   *   *

Old Mrs. Olson's only daughter came and lived in her house after she died in her sleep during a snowstorm on her 70th birthday. The daughter tended the Cornish Gilliflower apple tree and the Celsiana rose and all the cats for the rest of their long lives.

She was always a little puzzled, though, because she was just sure her mother had said she had a new kitten much like a long ago cat named Razzie. But she decided she must have been mistaken because there wasn't a black and white cat in the bunch. Nor did one ever again come to her door looking for a home.

Ann Gilson is a retired university librarian who has been active in animal rescue for more than sixty years. Her twin passions are books and cats, and she cares for a large collection of each.

4 PAWS AWARD

BRIGHTY

by Cynthia Bend

For my mother, birds supplied reliable wings up to the light and the beauty of life, a joy she made every effort to spread to her family and beyond. She kept close watch on her feathered friends, so was generally the first in our neighborhood to be informed of the latest bird news.

After an April storm, a neighbor called Mother with news of a fallen cedar in his front yard. "Looks like there's a nest in it. Some birds are screaming." His laconic comment may well have been enough to inform Mother that the loud-mouthed bird must have been a blue jay. She once told me of a brave jay parent who dive-bombed a cat away from its nest.

In that summer of 1958 our son Dick was ten, Harold five and Katie four. They were ripe for a voyage of discovery. I piled them into the bed of our jeep truck—no laws against it then—and we took the gravel road over Valley Creek toward the St. Croix River where we met Mother with little Doug and Susie Bianchi.

The nest was a shaggy collection of twigs scattered through the twisted branch of a fallen cedar. Bare-skinned, storm-soaked bird babies take no beauty prizes, and these fledglings were no exceptions, but I believe my mother saw them with their mama's eyes. Immediately she gathered them up and cradled them in her warm hands. She breathed out a long sad, "Ohoo." Then, "But one is still alive!" Pinfeathers were poking out of its loose skin, gray as death. Its squawks and gaping beak didn't add to its glamour. The five children crowded around Mother exhaling their warm breath over the baby, their bird-bright eyes sparking excitement.

The upshot of it was that we took home a new pet—something to add to the dog, the goat, the horses, and the chickens. Doug christened him "Brighty"—a name the scrawny hatchling needed time to grow into.

An easy way to keep Brighty happy and growing proved to be a diet of our chick starter moistened with water. The kids loaded their fingers, spitting on the grain when water wasn't handy. It seemed a sensible imitation of the mother jay. The kids stuffed the greedy beak as if they were raising a goose for *pate de foie gras,* and we adults did what we could to keep their nurturance from exploding the little bird like a popped balloon.

In his race to achieve adulthood before fall, Brighty soon outgrew his cage. My parents' philosophy of "room for one more" included Brighty, so he took up residence on their screened porch, much to the delight of Doug and Susie.

As the summer wore on, Brighty clung to his chickhood in spite of his brilliant blue plumage marked in black and scattered with pearls. He had imprinted on the nutrient-laden fingers of human birds, so stayed near his adopted flock. The boys often brought Brighty over to our house, frequently perched on Doug's head, claws tangled in his dark brown curls.

One day I decided it was time to give the dependent Brighty a lesson in food procurement. He and I were in the backyard near a great pile of sand, which Dick had amassed during his project of hole-digging. Brighty was perched on my shoulder. Nearby I spied a jade grasshopper. Brighty fluttered from my shoulder to the ground, definitely intrigued. He watched me move my hand closer … closer … still closer. His attention was riveted. As my thumb and forefinger stalked the insect, so did the beak of the beady-eyed Brighty. But—just as the capture seemed imminent, the grasshopper sprang, kicking Brighty in his feathered cheek. Brighty jumped backward, freeing the grasshopper to sing another day. I imagined he felt just how I'd feel if a hamburger jumped off my plate and kicked me.

By August Brighty was flying free, but never far from his adopted family. He had a habit of stealing bright objects. Six-year-old Harold was playing with a fuzzy toy mouse enlivened by a wire tail curved over its back so that, when wound up, the rotating tail turned the mouse over and over in the backyard dust. That bright key was a must-have for Brighty, and he swooped down, snatched it and hid it in his favorite spot under the shingles of our roof.

Another time my cousin Wells and I were standing in the back yard amiably chatting, Wells with a cigarette held lightly between his fingers, when Brighty catapulted from the sky, snatched the cigarette, fluttered to the roof, then tucked it with the key under the shingles—which fortunately were asphalt. I don't know whether he was trying to reform Wells, or he'd decided to take up the habit himself.

The last we heard of Brighty was from a family about four miles away. They were enjoying a fall picnic when suddenly a bird swooped down into the center of the feast and snatched his share of cake.

Cynthia Bend has trained dogs, horses and children separately and together. She is a writer whose latest book, Billy's Goat, *is based on two of her children's pets: a goat and a blue jay named Brighty. Cynthia would love to hear from you*: books@ cynthiabend.dgi.bz *or check her web site*: www.cynthiabend.dgi.bz.

BRIGHTY

Torry Bend

4 PAWS AWARD

REQUIEM FROM BUD FOR HIS MASTER

by Shirley Jean Coker

Dad:
>I know that sorrow fills a space,
>You close your eyes and see my face.
>You think of times I made you laugh,
>The love we shared, the bond we have.
>The special way I needed you,
>The friendship shared by just we two.
>I look down on you from up above,
>And wrap you in my thoughts of love.

Our paths will cross again Dad, Love,

Bud
June 30, 1996—January 6, 2006

Shirley Coker is retired from various professions, one of which was Veterinary Radiology and Vet Tech. She has raised and cared for animals her entire life.

THE GREAT CHICKEN RESCUE

by Craig William Andrews

There were times, usually unexpected times, when I believed that my dad had the fastest reflexes of any man in the whole world.

I was raised-up in a small town in southern California, and in those days it was still okay to keep chickens in your yard if you had a hankering to. We kept Bantams, and also a beautiful breed of very small chicken called Golden Seabrights.

As this story unfolds, it was an absolutely delicious day in early May—a warm and lazy afternoon. Dad was out puttering in the garden. Mom was fixing dinner, and I was out in the back hanging around my dad.

We had a very nice chicken coop in the corner of our yard, and that's where the chickens mostly stayed, except for Belinda, a little Banty hen. Whenever Dad would garden he would let Belinda out of the coop, and she would follow him around talking to him and eating the bugs that he would turn up for her. I think she really loved him, and I think, in his own way, my dad felt the same.

There was a large expanse of undeveloped hills that bordered our town, and wild things lived there. Coyotes, fox, raccoon, and even an occasional bobcat, would find their way to where we lived. Some of our neighbors had lost a chicken or two, but we had a dog, and we never had any trouble. That day, however, trouble did come, and it came, quite literally, "from out of the blue."

Dad was bent down with his back to me loosening up the soil from around the rose bushes. Belinda was about six or seven feet from him, pecking around a rock, and I was sitting on the grass petting our dog. Next thing I knew, a very large hawk came in from behind me, right over the top of my head, grabbed up Belinda, and was carrying her off!

I mean, we are now talking the stuff of legends—of epics—of Great Historical Events! I was nine years old, sitting in my backyard in South Pasadena, California, where everybody is safe, when a *huge* hawk flies right over the top of my head, totally ignoring both me and my courageous dog, and hauls off my favorite chicken right before my eyes! This does not happen! My eyes were big, and my mouth was hanging open in silent, gaping disbelief. And then my dad—*My Dad*—suddenly whirls around, unwinds like a top, leaps into the air, and grabs Belinda right out of the talons of a flying hawk. *Wow!* And you should've seen the look on that hawk's face. He let out a squawk, flapped his wings like he had just gotten hit with a rock, and hightailed it out of there just as fast as he could fly. In fact, he was still squawking when he cleared our neighbor's roof and disappeared from sight. And Belinda? She was hysterical! I didn't think we were ever going to get her calmed down again. But she did live into a ripe old age, and I'm sure she told her chicks all about it.

Craig Andrews is a Registered Counselor who lives with his wife in Port Angeles, Washington. They live with four geese and a duck named Bud, two rowdy farm dogs, and two overly dramatic cats, one of which (Mr. Wilson) is a foster cat who refused to leave.

4 PAWS AWARD
Best Nonfiction

MURPHY BROWN ... AND BLACK AND WHITE

by Kim McBride

Neither our friends nor our family could ever understand why in the world we loved our little wirehaired fox terrier so much. She was seldom affectionate. She was often dirty. She was always ill-mannered. But I guess you had to be there to understand. We had any number of nicknames for that dog over the fourteen years she graced our lives, but probably the most accurate was "Bad Attitude."

I had always wanted a wirehaired fox terrier. As a child I had seen old reruns of "The Thin Man" in which the starring couple, Nick and Nora, had an intriguing little wirehaired fox terrier named Asta. I swore that someday I would have a dog like that, and yesireee, by golly, I got one, and guess what—she was just like that dog Asta, because now that I think about it, what made him so interesting and funny was his "bad attitude." He was always doing something naughty.

She was a darling puppy. She was mostly white with just a few spots of brown and black. When naming her, we were again influenced by a TV series, one that had been extremely popular a few years before called "Murphy Brown." Of course we had to adapt her name, so she became Murphy Brown ... and Black and White, but Murphy for short.

What was so misleading about this adorable little puppy was that she was so well behaved. Every puppy I've had in the past always pitched a fit for the first couple of nights when they were left alone. Not her. We would put her in a box, and she would lie down and immediately go to sleep without a peep. She didn't bark, she never whined, and it only took me one day to house train her. She didn't pull any of the usual naughty puppy tricks. She didn't chew our shoes or the furniture. She didn't dig up our back yard, and she never in her whole life got into the trash, not even when it was full of chicken bones. I should have known she was too good to be true.

Murphy was indeed the perfect puppy, until one day when she was about eight months old. That's when her true identity began to emerge. Yes, that was the day I thought I had put away all the groceries, but unfortunately I had left a package of sixteen rolls of toilet paper sitting on the rug in the living room. We went away for a few hours, and Murphy, being so perfect, was allowed to remain in the house. Upon arriving home, we found Murphy innocently sleeping on the couch, no doubt in need of some rest. There was nothing left that even remotely resembled sixteen rolls of toilet paper. Instead there were torn up bits of tissue everywhere. The pieces measured anywhere from the size of a dime to a few feet in length. The really amazing thing was that each piece was almost exactly three inches apart, all over the entire house. You would have thought someone had spent days, ruler in hand, measuring out the distance between each little piece. It was too much for our vacuum cleaner. We had to crawl around on the floor for hours picking it all up by hand. The words "Murphy" and "perfect" were never again mentioned in the same sentence.

There are two things that are constantly repeated in descriptions of wirehaired fox terriers. One is "tenacious" which means persistent and stubborn. The other is that they are "bred for catching vermin." The definition of vermin is "troublesome small animals e.g. squirrels, rats, and gophers." Murphy's problem was she took those descriptions to a whole new level. The older she got the more tenacious she became in her pursuit of vermin. Unfortunately her definition of vermin was: every animal, large or small and even inanimate objects if someone was moving them, such as shovels, hoes, rakes, tractor tires, chainsaws, etc.

The first vermin she attempted to catch and destroy was my large white feather duster. Rather than being feathery, it was white and fluffy. Or, as Murphy would have said, white and rabbit-like. I could never again dust, or for that matter vacuum, when she was in the same room.

Even though Murphy hated vermin, she did like people, and we chose to think she loved us. Of course, we may have been wrong, because every chance she got, she tried to escape from us. She was extremely quick and agile, and one day she managed to slip past us and out the front door.

Murphy took off in a dead run, but not into the street as I had feared. Instead she ran along each fence and house, silently and swiftly seeking out vermin all the way down the block. I jumped into my van and drove down the street yelling out the window for her to come back. After the first block I realized that terriers can't hear when they escape. Apparently their noses go to the ground (in pursuit of vermin), and we can only theorize that this causes their ears to close up because they become completely oblivious to all calling, screaming, begging, bribing, and cussing that ensues.

It dawned on me that I should get the duster since she'd never been able to resist it. I drove home, grabbed the duster, sped back down the street, rolled down my window and swung that white duster back and forth with all my might. Murphy came running, got about two feet away from me, realized it was a trick, and turned around and took off again. I only caught her because she finally found some other dogs (vermin) on the other side of someone's backyard fence and became so engrossed in trying to get to them I was able to sneak up on her. I often wondered what all those people thought who saw the wacko woman driving her van down the street yelling and swinging a duster out her car window.

When Murphy was two years old we bought a house on a few acres, nestled in a little valley between two mountain ranges. The day we moved in Murphy managed to escape. The last I saw of her, her nose was to the ground, her ears were shut, and she was heading for the hills at about thirty miles per hour. The foothills next to our property were covered in sagebrush and home to numerous coyotes. Coyotes who would gleefully welcome a little guest for dinner. Murphy was heading away from the few houses that were near us, so even though she had a new identification tag on, I didn't hold much hope of her ever being seen again. I was distraught, picturing her dying of thirst or being torn to bits by the coyotes, and I took to my bed, alternately crying and praying for her safe return. A few hours later the phone rang. It was a gentleman who lived about a half mile away on the top of a hill. He said he had caught our dog. It seemed she was once again trying to get at some vermin (his dog in his backyard) and was so distracted he was able to catch her.

Murphy loved living in the country. The back half of our property was part of a mountain and home to numerous vermin, and Murphy delighted in the chase. We grew vegetables to sell at a farmers' market so even though we were animal lovers and hated to see any animal killed, we appreciated the way Murphy controlled the gopher and squirrel population. There's nothing like seeing a large plant you've grown from seed disappearing down a gopher hole to make you decide there are some exceptions. Most of the time she brought the victims (I mean vermin) in and placed them precisely in the middle of our living room rug for a viewing. Though we weren't pleased with her presentation, we had to praise her for doing what she considered to be her one and only job in life.

Murphy always barked like crazy at aircraft. We lived in an area near where planes were built and tested, so they flew over often. Whenever someone would remark about Murphy barking at planes, my husband would say, "Yup, she's one hell of a watchdog. Not once has any airplane ever attempted to land in our yard."

About a year after we moved, Murphy pulled off her third escape. I don't recall exactly how it came about, but I do recall seeing Murphy running down the road, nose to the ground and ears shut again. A neighbor later described the scene—"She went by so fast she looked like a fifty foot long dog flying by." We searched all over for her, but to no avail. At least this time she was headed towards some houses so I thought there might be hope of someone finding her. Once again, I took to my bed alternately crying and praying for her safe return. A few hours later the phone rang, and a child's voice asked me if I had lost my dog. He told me he had found her chasing his dog. Knowing Murphy's desire to kill all creatures great and small, I prayed the entire time I drove to his home in hopes that Murphy hadn't injured his dog. When I got to his yard, there he was, a boy of about five, holding tightly onto Murphy. He scolded me, saying, "Your dog chased my dog all over the yard. My dog was so scared he had his tail between his legs." I glanced over and saw that his dog was a very large and beautiful German Shepherd. I gave the boy a reward and left, grateful the German Shepherd was still alive and in one piece.

After we had lived on our little farm for a few years, we decided to buy a couple of horses. We were extremely worried about Murphy and her desire to kill vermin but hoped the mere size of a horse would be a deterrent. The day our first horse arrived, we kept Murphy locked in our backyard. She watched intently as the horse was unloaded and then started barking like crazy. I stood next to the horse waiting while my husband let Murphy out. She came running full speed up the hill toward the horse. I held my breath in fear that she would immediately go for one of the horse's legs. I tried to read the expression on her face in order to prepare for what might happen next. At about fifty yards her expression was intense, she was definitely going in for the kill. At about twenty-five yards the horse must have started looking bigger because her speed started to slow just slightly. I noted her expression was beginning to change. At five feet I read her expression as saying "holy crap!" as she put on the brakes, coming to an abrupt halt right next to one of the horse's front legs. She stood there in awe. Her eyes moved slowly, taking it all in, beginning at the horse's hooves and continuing to its head. Finally she turned around and, looking quite dejected, slowly walked away making a sort of low grumbling-growling sound that I would definitely describe as cussing under her breath.

I considered it a defeat. Murphy, however, only considered it a mild setback. She bided her time. She waited until she found the horse lying down in the pasture. She snuck up behind him, slowly stalking her prey. Then suddenly she made a mad leap for the back of his neck, gave him a nip and then turned and trotted proudly away with, what I would swear was, a wily smile on her face. Apparently she considered him conquered since she never again attempted to bite him.

She did love to chase the horses, however. Occasionally we would let them out of their corrals, and they would run down the hill to where we had a nice green pasture for them to graze. As they ran, she would join in, running right behind their hind feet, barking and pretending that they were running because they were afraid of her. We would always cringe for fear she would one day irritate the horses enough that they would try to kick the little idiot's head in. And one day one of them did!

I remember hearing my husband yelling that Murphy had been kicked, and we needed to get her to the vet. He said when he got to her, she was lying there jerking and staring blankly. It was a half hour drive into town, and I knew she would die in my arms on the way. I told him I couldn't bear to go, so he set off alone. Once again I took to my bed. I cried the entire time they were gone. Finally he returned, and when he came into the house she wasn't with him. My heart sank. I knew she was dead. I tearfully asked what had happened. He said she just lay there in the seat jerking all the way into town. Then as he pulled up to the vet's, she suddenly jumped up and acted just fine. I asked him if he'd left her at the vet's. He said, "No, she's outside chasing some birds."

The score was now: horses—two, Murphy—one. She found a way to even that score. We lived near the desert so most of the year it was hot. Since she spent a lot of time running around hunting for vermin, she would get quite warm. We got her a washtub and filled it with water so she could cool off, but she wasn't interested.

Even though it was much harder to get into and out of, she much preferred cooling off in the horses' water trough. On some extremely hot days, she would go for a little swim at least four times a day. I figured the horses' punishment for kicking her in the head was having to drink dog-flavored water. The score was now even.

Since Murphy had managed to co-exist with the horses without killing them, my uncle decided to get us three baby goats. He thought he was being cute. We thought the baby goats were cute. Murphy thought the baby goats were cute … vermin. We built a sturdy fence for them but lived in fear Murphy would somehow get in. We decided to try to make her understand that she was not to hurt them. At first she would just stare at them and run back and forth next to their fence. We knew exactly what she wanted to do to them. But with a lot of hard work, we finally seemed to get through to her.

Over time Murphy developed a coping skill that allowed her occasionally to overcome her bad attitude and to actually deal with vermin without eradicating them. She would, however, only use this skill if you were within choking range of her. Here's how it worked: Murphy would psych herself into pretending the vermin didn't exist.

One time I enrolled her in obedience class. I threatened her for ten minutes in the car before the first class. Once we entered the room, I held her tightly in my arms until the class started. When I finally had to put her down, I held my breath. Every time she started to go after a dog, I jerked her leash and yelled at her. Amazingly, she suddenly composed herself and trotted around the ring like all the other dogs. The only difference was that she stared straight ahead, a totally disgusted look on her face and made that low grumbling, growling (cussing) noise she made whenever she was mad. She really only learned two things in that class: 1) how to sit and 2) if you can't kill it, pretend it doesn't exist.

She employed this same psychology whenever we visited the vet. I would give her the usual lecture in the car, "no bad attitude and no killing or maiming." I would carry her into the waiting room and head directly to the chair furthest from any other animal in the room. I would then hold her in my lap with one hand on her leash and the other with a white-knuckled grip on her collar. If an animal passed by within ear-shredding range, we'd both tense up. I'd grab her collar with both hands, but then to my surprise, she would just stare straight ahead and not even acknowledge there was another animal in the room. This from the dog who'd run circles in our van every time she saw another dog through the window. Circles that went from the floor, to the seat, to the top of the seat and over, down to the floor, up and over the next seat, into my lap and over my shoulder while I was driving, all the while jumping and barking obnoxiously. Often she would do this when she saw a rock in the middle of a field that mildly resembled an animal.

The goats stretched Murphy's coping ability. Those three goats were great at keeping down the weeds in their pen. But we had a fenced-in area at the top of our property that was full of weeds and posed a fire hazard. The problem was getting the goats from their pen to the weeds. At first we would lock Murphy up, and one of us would lead the goats, tempting them with a bucket of oats, while the other person kept the goats moving along from behind. This worked for a while, until the goats realized that if they just ran away they could eat out of the delicious salad bar I called my garden. We tried many different scenarios but finally decided there was only one way to get them up there. We would drive them up in our old Dodge pickup. For a variety of reasons, loading them in the back of the truck didn't work. So one day we decided to try loading the goats into the front of the truck. Murphy was with us, and she hated those goats, but even though there were three goats, two people, and one dog all in the front seat of that old pickup truck, she managed to sit quietly in my lap, staring straight ahead, enduring both the foul smell and the constant jostling. I was so proud of her. At last, we had found a way to get the goats to the weeds and back safely— well, as safely as driving up and down a steep hill with three constantly moving goats in your front seat can be.

Murphy put up with the horses and the goats, but that was her limit. One night we came home late, and all the lights were turned off in the house. As we came though our front door, we heard a commotion in the kitchen/dining room. At first we froze, sure it was an intruder. Something was moving all about the large room, knocking into furniture and making weird noises. At last I was able to make out what it was. It was Murphy, and in that semi-darkness it looked as though she was staggering around, bumping into walls and furniture. I thought, "Oh my God, either she's been kicked in the head again or has suffered a debilitating stroke." My heart sank in my chest. We finally got the lights turned on. It was Murphy all right. She was running around the room with a snake in her mouth. She treated it just like she treated her ball. She would jump up in the air, arching her entire body one direction, and then while in mid-air quickly arch in the opposite direction, letting go of the snake at precisely the right moment to send it flying. It would try to slither away or hide under something, but she would catch it just in time and run joyfully around the room before flinging it once more. I'd never seen her happier. We finally got the snake away from her. Murphy was all right, though disappointed. The snake was all right, I hope. I was not all right. I was traumatized by the whole episode, especially when I realized the snake could easily have been a rattlesnake instead of a king snake. It could have gotten away from her, slithered under our couch or our bed and been waiting there for us when we came home.

Thank God Murphy never brought another snake into the house, at least not one we ever found. She did, however, have a very close encounter with a rattlesnake. I was working in the garden when I heard her having a fit up in the horse barn. At first I thought she was just barking at a rabbit or a squirrel. Then I remembered it was summer and the height of rattlesnake season, and took off running for the barn. Sure enough, when I arrived I found her with a very large rattler cornered between some bales of hay. She kept jumping at it, and it kept striking at her. I was petrified. I didn't know what to do. If I tried to grab her, the snake would probably get me. I kept calling her, but of course she ignored me. I yelled at the top of my lungs for my husband, hoping he was outside and would hear me. All I could think of was that Murphy was going to die. Then for some reason Murphy backed away and ran past me and out one of the barn doors. I couldn't believe it! I had never seen her leave an animal alone when she was in her "killing vermin" mode. Amazed, I just stood there staring at the snake and thanking God for letting Murphy live, when back she came through the opposite barn door, charged past me and resumed attacking the snake. The idiot. Shortly, my husband arrived, grabbed a shovel and used it to push Murphy far enough back from the rattler so I could grab her.

Another day I'll never forget occurred when Murphy and I were traveling on a winding, mountainous road on the way home from the groomer. Just as we approached a hairpin curve near the top of the mountain, I saw a police officer putting out flares. He said there had been a very bad accident right around the curve, and they were waiting for a medivac helicopter. I pulled over and volunteered to tell oncoming drivers so they could turn around if they wanted. I stood there for half an hour until someone relieved me so I could get a drink from my van. I forgot all about Murphy when I opened the door, and out she went. She ran around the curve with me in pursuit. She ran through the crowd at the accident scene, then off the edge of the road and down a steep ravine next to a hill. There was absolutely nothing I could do. I couldn't run after her; she was long gone. I couldn't use my car to try to find her because the helicopter still hadn't arrived. There weren't even any houses around so that someone might find her. I knew this was the end of Murphy Brown and Black and White. I stood there in a daze, amongst the paramedics, the firemen, and the crowd of people who'd gathered. Forty-five minutes later, from the opposite side of the hill, up over the edge of the road popped Murphy. It was unbelievable. She had run completely around the entire hill (about three quarters of a mile) and unbeknownst to her, ended up right back where she started from. I knew exactly what she was thinking by the happy look on her face. She'd run around to the backside of the hill, far enough so that she could no longer hear the noise of the accident scene. Then as she progressed around the hill, she started hearing voices and headed toward them. She figured where there were voices, there might be other dogs (vermin). I saw the look of shock on her face when she recognized me among the crowd. She started to take off again, but I yelled, "Catch that dog," and a fireman did. There was a lot of grumbling-growling (cussing) sound coming from my car on the way home, but this time it was coming from me.

Despite all the escape attempts, I knew Murphy loved us. Whenever I was feeling down she would come to me and stare deep into my eyes. It was as though she were trying to communicate with me so she could comfort me. I felt a connection with her I've never felt with any other animal. She was very spoiled. She had my husband and me so well trained if she jumped up on the bed, even if we were sound asleep, we'd both automatically lift up the covers so she could get into bed with us.

It's been a year now since she died, and I miss her so much. She may have been a dog with a "bad attitude," but I don't think a day ever went by when she didn't make us laugh. She was a very special dog who lived hard and fast, *tenaciously* seeking out *vermin* until the day she died.

Kim McBride is a retired Superior Courtroom Clerk who enjoys dabbling in all forms of art and gardening. She lives in Sequim, Washington, with her husband John and two Welsh Terriers, Nigel and Archibald.

© Raven 2007

MAKE MY DAY

Raven O'Keefe

4 PAWS AWARD

Dogs

by Linda Wentz

My God, dogs are disgusting! Shuffling about with their tongues hanging out … drooling … reeking of decomposed gym socks.

Alas, I am obliged to make an arduous study of these repulsive creatures since the people I live with possess two eighty-pound collies.

These two crude beasts, I am confident, are of the male gender. They expose themselves by the manner in which they casually raise one leg, tip ever so slightly to one side—and pee! I am convinced that dogs will pee anywhere, everywhere and on anything, as if it were some sort of compulsive disorder. In fact, I've come to believe that peeing is a dog's single most important function in life, other than barking at imagined friends and foes. Of course, neither of the vile creatures is toilet-trained—which, given their ages, I find inexcusable. I've stopped counting the times I have meandered through our flowerbeds only to happen upon a randomly deposited pile of … well, you know … out in the open for all to see. No pooper scoopers here!

And always underfoot. People get up, dogs get up. People go for a walk; dogs go for a walk.… Now you have a clue why Fido is so often named Shadow.

Such humiliating displays of servility are shameful to relate, and I am of the opinion all of "dogdumb" may exhibit the same abject behavior.

I did try, in the beginning, to communicate with my roomies. However, I found their conversation all too often goes something like this: "Slippers? Me get slippers! Paper? Get paper! Ball? Run, chase! Me catch. EEEHAW!"

Occasionally they provide the family—especially me—amusement. Case in point: One day, Hairball Number One, looking a bit green around the gums, declined a game of Frisbee. I quickly switched to the weather channel to see if Hell had, indeed, frozen over. But it turned out Number One had not attended the Lassie Learning Center and had drunk from the toilet bowl.

Sadly, the poor things haven't a clue how pitifully comical they appear. Oh, and did I mention breath? Hot gusts of halitosis … fetid slime dripping from gaping mouths.… The mere thought makes the hair on my neck stand straight up. Keeps me up most of the night!

You may ask how a celebrity such as me—dignified, tidy, and cerebral—is able to survive such frequent assaults upon my sensibilities. Being generous, albeit aloof, I try to remember that dogs are simply scavengers doing what comes naturally. I keep to myself and the two hairballs give me a wide berth.

Wait a minute. What's this? The sun has moved. I must relocate. I will continue this another time.

Best regards,
The Cat

Linda Wentz is a retired homemaker who graduated from Peninsula College in 2001. "Dogs" was written in memory of Ladd, Wolf and Miss Moppet, beloved pets for nearly 23 years.

4 PAWS AWARD

CATS A-PLENTY

by Sally M. Harris

I'm blessed with cats a-plenty,
as many as I can find.
I love them each to pieces,
I'm not the monogamous kind.

No discrimination on my part,
any feline will do.
Affection, food, a cozy bed,
my furry friends' needs are few.

Devon Rex, Siamese, or street cats
are equally appealing.
On a cold and desperate night
their love is warm and healing.

I don't mind when they sleep all day
leaving stray fur here and there.
All I ask is they please not spray.
I think that's only fair.

Sally M. Harris resides in Sequim, Washington, with her husband, Allan, and Devon Rex cat, Lily of the Nile. She is the author of the newly released children's book, The Caterpillar's Dream. *Sally dedicates her poem to the many cats that have touched her heart.*

DAY DREAMING GEORGIE

Nancy O'Gorman

SEARCHING

by Ann Gilson

Marnie wasn't a particularly attractive little girl. Only eight, she was thin and slight, with mousy blond hair and a few freckles, and wary eyes.

Nor was Golightly a showy chicken, being a Rhode Island Red with a regrettable mixture of Leghorn. This had the unfortunate effect of reducing her brain power, increasing her flightiness, and giving her a somewhat mongrel appearance.

Marnie loved her anyhow, and was glad as she crept through the alley that neither of them was memorable alone. Unfortunately, as a couple they were noticeable. That's why she kept Golightly clasped tightly to her chest under her jacket as she hurried along.

Fear nibbled at the edges of her mind as she left the alley behind the house where she had spent nearly all the years she could remember and moved down the sidewalk, heading west and keeping to the shadows as she passed the streetlights that occasionally cast a circle of light along the street.

Past the Smiths, the Derwenters and the Simpsons. Then the school she attended each fall. *No more,* she thought as she hurried along. A few more blocks and no more houses she knew. She relaxed a little, and Golightly stirred sleepily as the pressure of Marnie's arm around her eased.

Marnie slowed down, but remained on guard, as she reviewed her plans, and the steps she'd taken.

As far back as she could remember she and Crystal had been alone. She had never called Crystal "Mom" or "Mother"——no one who looked at Crystal would have. Soft and sweet and trusting, Crystal was fatally beautiful and congenitally stupid. Marnie loved Crystal, but she had no illusions about her, and when Rick entered their lives she knew there would be trouble.

Though she and Crystal had always lived alone, within weeks of meeting Crystal, Rick had moved in with them. He hardly noticed Marnie, besotted as he was with Crystal. But after a few months he began making little changes that increased his comfort. Crystal was compliant but Marnie was not, and soon she was aware that Rick saw her as an enemy.

She was not really a match for him, and when he had announced at supper-time that he and Crystal had talked it over and decided that Golightly would have to go, she realized that her only option was flight.

He explained in his pleasant, reasonable way that having a chicken in the house was unsanitary and aggravated his allergies, and that her clucking at odd hours was disruptive of their rest. He would take Golightly to the animal shelter in the morning, where she would no doubt find a loving home, preferably in the country.

Crystal chimed in with, "I know you're fond of her, honey, but like Ricky says, a house is really no place for a chicken. They'll find her a place where she can have a regular chicken life and she'll be happy." Marnie nodded and held her tears back until she went up to her bedroom, where she sobbed quietly on a sleepy Golightly's soft feathers.

Then she blew her nose and washed her face and sat on the bed to decide what to do. Letting Rick take Golightly away was not to be considered. *In somebody's stew pot,* she thought, knowing Rick. But what could she do? She and Crystal had no friends, really, and no family that she knew of. It would be useless to approach a teacher, a neighbor, a social worker. They would not see Rick's demand as unreasonable.

Ever since kindhearted Crystal had let her bring Golightly home when school was out three years ago, an Easter class pet as a fluffy chick and unwanted as a gangly teenager by the end of May, she had been Marnie's best friend and dearest consolation. Her slight limp, caused by careless handling in the classroom, and her less than stellar appearance made Marnie more fiercely protective of her. Marnie knew Rick wanted Golightly dead, and suspected that she herself would be the next to be banished.

She got up and took her shower then, but instead of changing into her paja-mas she quietly began to pack her school backpack, unloading her school things and putting them away neatly. She put in clean underwear and socks, a pair of jeans and a couple of shirts, a sweater, comb, soap and other personal stuff, a pen-cil and notepad, and Band-Aids, a couple pounds of Golightly's "chicken scratch" food from the sack in the closet, and a water container. The night was cool, though it was early June, so she dressed in jeans, a long sleeved T-shirt, a light jacket, a safari hat, her good walking shoes, and stuffed gloves in one pocket.

Before she turned out the light she took a piece of paper from the tablet on her desk, wrote "Don't worry about us, Crystal. We'll be alright. I love you. Marnie" and put it on her pillow. Then she turned out the light, tucked Golightly under her arm, and walked very quietly down the dark hallway, past Crystal and Rick's room, and downstairs to the kitchen.

Without turning on a light she quickly put half a loaf of bread, a chunk of cheese, grapes and an apple, and a handful of cookies in a sack. Last, she stood for a few seconds looking out the window. Then, having made up her mind, she lifted down a canister of macaroni, felt around inside it and withdrew a baggie filled with money. Marnie had no idea how much it held—Crystal usually kept less than $100 in emergency money there. It didn't matter, and she took it all. She would need it. She put it in her backpack, put the backpack on her back, and left the only home she could really remember, Golightly in her arms.

And now, two hours later, she was nearing the edge of town. There were more and more vacant lots, and sometimes whole blocks (or what would have been blocks) were vacant. She was nearing the small airport outside of town, and now she needed to find shelter for what remained of the night.

Right ahead was a hangar/shed for a small private aircraft, the farthest one from the terminal. The airplane was locked, so she put Golightly on a strut to roost and lay down beside her, backpack under her head for a pillow. As she slipped into sleep her last thought was "I'll go to Miz Rich or to the angels."

*   *   *   *

George Morgan woke with a pounding headache, an all too frequent event during the past year. After he found his way to the bathroom, eyes slitted against the early morning light, and swallowed a couple of aspirin, he sank into a chair by the window and looked out at the Seattle skyline. It was clear but there were some low-hanging gray clouds, threatening later rain. He thought, for the umpteenth time, how well the sky and his mood matched.

George didn't look like he felt. He was a relatively young man, still slender, well-muscled and with a full head of sandy hair. Fairly tall, regular features, not especially memorable unless he smiled, which he seldom did these days. By all objective measures, he should have smiled a lot.

He was healthy, an inheritance some years ago left him free to pursue whatever work or pleasure he chose, he held a prestigious degree, had an excellent mind, and possessed amiable family connections and numerous interesting friends.

What George didn't have, and the reason for his self-pity this morning, as well as his unfortunate overindulgence the night before—many nights before, in fact—was a wife. More than that, except for the wife who had left him a year ago, George had never found anyone whom he thought he loved and wanted to spend a lifetime with.

Looking back, as he did nearly every morning, he could see that he'd been mistaken about his love for Sherri. She'd been mistaken, too, for he didn't have as much money as she'd thought he did, and when she realized this, she very sensibly left him and started hunting again. Her kind of looks don't last long and she couldn't afford to waste any time.

He should be grateful she'd been so forthright, George realized, but the whole thing had shaken his confidence. Now he wondered, if by some chance he found someone and fell in love again, whether he'd have the courage to take another chance. He hoped to hell so! The thought of living alone for a lifetime made a chill run down his spine.

To get rid of it he got up and made coffee and toast, then went out onto the apartment balcony and tried to decide what to do today. The clouds were breaking up and a few more rays of sunshine peeked through. It was still very early, for the sun comes up very early in June so far north.

He felt a sudden urge to get out of the city, to shake his mood and fears off and head somewhere—anywhere—at high speed. He'd go out to the little airport some thirty miles away, where he kept his plane, and just take off. He didn't really care where to, he could decide that when he got ready to file a flight plan. Maybe the San Juan Islands, or Victoria, or maybe south to Oregon. Just get moving.

He quickly put his dishes in the dishwasher, showered and dressed, packed an overnight satchel "in case," closed doors and windows, checked that he had keys, wallet, checkbook, and headed downstairs to the parking area.

His car was warmed by the now full sunlight as he slid into it, turned the key, moved smoothly into traffic and headed for Pinetree and the airport. His mood lightened and he felt almost cheerful now that he was on his way.

*   *   *   *

Whitney Fairfield wondered how much longer she'd be staying in Port Angeles as she unlocked the door of the small, and very successful, gift shop she'd opened a little over two years ago. Her assistant wouldn't be in until 10:00, and the store didn't open until 9:30, but Whitney loved to have this first hour alone each day. She started coffee in the little back office/storeroom, unwrapped the bran muffin she'd picked up at Elizabeth and Co., and sat in the comfortable chair at her desk while the coffee brewed. Then she poured a cupful and ate her still warm muffin while she planned her day at the shop.

Anyone watching her might have wondered what such a young woman was doing in the back room of a tiny shop in a small and rather isolated city. Seeing her on the streets of a large city, one would have taken her for a very expensive model or actress, perhaps, although she was more classically beautiful than is currently fashionable and was more feminine in outline. She sat, and moved, with a completely unconscious assurance that betrayed generations of success behind her. Her reading glasses, perched now on her nose as she made out a list of things to do today, helped disguise the quite formidable intelligence in her eyes.

Well, what was she doing here, and how much longer would she stay? As she asked herself that question she took off her glasses and stared unseeingly through the door at the shop window blind, still pulled down against the sun. Her shoulders slumped a little as she thought back to two and a half years ago, when she decided to come here on the latest leg of the search that had started a little over five years ago.

Whitney knew better than to think back to the beginning, but she could manage two and a half years okay, she thought. The detective's kind, ugly face and his sympathetic eyes—his voice saying, "Miss Fairfield, the trail ended in Port Angeles" played again in her mind, as it had that day in his office, high above the traffic in Seattle.

"I've followed your friend back almost ten years, through several jobs, name changes, and living arrangements. But ten years ago, when she and her mother appeared in Port Angeles, the trail stops. I can find no trace of either of them before that time. The mother, if that is who she was, stayed on for a year after Diane left and then she disappeared."

He leaned back, waited for her to speak, and then went on, "One thing stands out in Port Angeles that I didn't find in any of the other places Diane lived. She told several people she worked with there that, 'If I ever have a family this is where I'd want to live. It's a wonderful place for children.' So far as I know, she never spoke of having children to anyone after she left Port Angeles. Perhaps that's where she learned she would never have any."

The detective, John Pilkington, waited while Whitney thought. When she finally spoke, "Is there anything more you can do?" he answered "I don't believe so." Then he added, "Not now. Not that would be worth the money you'd spend. But your daughter will be starting kindergarten next fall. It's possible that Diane will take her to Port Angeles and raise her there. If she does, she will probably change her own name, her appearance, and get a job unrelated to the one she held there before. She may even change the child's appearance, if possible."

So she'd come to Port Angeles, Whitney thought, she'd opened the shop, bought a house, changed her name though she couldn't do much about her face, and volunteered at the schools, the "Y," and the Girl Scouts. She'd cultivated an acquaintance with almost every person in town who worked with children.

Although Marguerite was only three when she and Diane disappeared together, Whitney had never doubted that she would know her daughter if—no, when—she found her. And though Diane was evidently almost professional when it came to changing her appearance, Whitney was pretty sure she'd recognize her voice if she heard it—and she never stopped listening for it.

But she had not found either of them, and she felt more and more sure that she would have if they were anywhere in the area. The shop itself was a sort of bait, carrying many items to delight a little girl, plus all the things Whitney remembered Diane being drawn to.

Whitney had even hired her assistant so that she herself could remain in the screened off back room working, but could hear the customers being waited on. Once she'd been sure she heard Diane's voice, but the woman turned out to be a local, married the past twenty years to one of the town's ministers. Perhaps it was time to try something else, though she couldn't think what. She knew she would keep looking, perhaps for a lifetime.

*   *   *   *

When George drew up at the airport the coffee shop wasn't open yet, so he decided to walk down to the little hangar/shed where his plane was tied down. It was the last one in the row and quite a way, but it felt good to stretch his legs. The grass was wet and his overnight bag was heavier than he'd thought, and he'd begun to wish he'd waited a bit. But he was there now, and he turned around the end of the building, intending to toss his bag in the plane and then taxi back to the terminal area.

As he swung around the corner, he stopped in mid-stride and his mouth fell open. He felt as dazed as he looked, for there on a wing strut sat a chicken, fixing him with a beady eye.

Good Lord, chickens really do have beady eyes! he thought. The chicken ominously began to cackle, low at first then louder and more furiously. He was sure the chicken was going to launch herself at him, when a body rolled out from under the plane and a child's startled voice said, "Golightly, hush! Hush, girl!" and the chicken subsided.

The girl, small and self-possessed, came to her feet, brushing herself off and straightening her rumpled clothes. She examined him carefully for a moment, then making up her mind, she held out her hand and said, "I'm Marnie and this is Golightly. You must be the owner of this plane."

As he took her small hand in his, George was warmed by her friendliness and trust, partly because he sensed that for her, trust was selective. He set down his bag and said, "I'm George, and yes, this is my plane, but," he added jokingly, "You're welcome to use it for a roost," this last to Golightly.

Golightly moved down the strut and turned her head to look at him, then jumped down and walked to Marnie, where she made a churring sound in her throat. Marnie picked up her pack, took out the baggie of chicken scratch and poured a small pile of it on the ground, then set down the small container of water and removed the lid. Golightly promptly ate breakfast.

George and Marnie moved away slightly and George, who'd had a few minutes to think the situation over, asked casually, "And how do you and Golightly find yourselves sleeping at the airport this morning?"

Marnie, sounding much older than she appeared to be, said, "It is a bit of a surprise to find a chicken and a girl when you expected only a plane, isn't it? I suppose I'd better explain. Let's sit down."

So they moved a piece of crating out into the sun, sat down, and Marnie continued, "When I was very little, Crystal (that's my mom) used to say, 'If things get too bad we can always go back to Miz Rich, or maybe to the port of the angels.'

"I don't know why, but I remember crying a lot when I was really little. And she always used to say that. Then somehow I didn't cry anymore—I wasn't a baby, I guess—and she didn't say it anymore. But I always remembered it, and used to say it to myself sometimes. Like when Crystal had a boyfriend who was mean to her, or we ran out of money, or she didn't come home and I had to go look for her.

"Things have been better the last couple of years, until Rick moved in. He hates me, really hates me. Then last night he said, all smarmy and sweet, that 'they' had decided to take Golightly to the animal shelter where she'd get a nice home in the country. Crystal really believes that—she's not very smart. But he wants Golightly dead, and he wants to be rid of me."

George made a small sympathetic sound, and Marnie's voice trembled a second as she went on, "So I remembered what Crystal said and since things were about as bad as they could be, I decided to find Miz Rich or the port of the angels. Now I've got to figure out where they are and then go find them." She sighed.

Golightly politely went to the edge of the grass, relieved herself and returned. Marnie patted her head absently.

George, who'd kept his eyes on her while she spoke, now looked toward the terminal building, where a small commuter plane was just landing, and asked seriously, "Do you have any idea how to find either of them?"

"I thought about it walking out here last night," Marnie replied, "and I have no idea who 'Miz Rich' is or where she might be. I don't think that's her real name, anyway. Crystal used to say 'Miz Rich Bitch' once in a while, too, so I think it was like a nickname. And I don't think she was really a friend of Crystal's either. Crystal doesn't have any women friends now, and she's never mentioned her since I was little. She may not even be real. Crystal makes things up sometimes." This last was said matter-of-factly.

Then her face brightened. "But I do have an idea about the port of the angels. When I was little I thought it was a sort of porthole in the clouds that the angels used to go in and out of Heaven, but that was silly. I think maybe it's a real place. Crystal sometimes makes little jokes like calling the garage 'the house of the car.'

"There's a boy, Miguel his name is, who was in my class at school this last year. He came about Easter and when the teacher introduced him, she said he came from Port Angeles. He laughed and said there weren't many angels in that port and he liked it better here. I didn't know what he was talking about and didn't pay any attention. Boys! But last night that popped into my mind and I think he meant that Port Angeles is port of the angels in Mexican." She looked up hopefully at George.

George was surprised at his surprise. This was a very bright kid. He nodded slowly. "I think you are right," he said. "So, now what?"

"I've got some money, but I haven't counted it yet," she said. "If there's enough, I'll get a plane ticket. If not, we can walk. I've got plenty of time and I like to walk." She turned and opened her pack, rooted around and drew out the plastic bag full of bills. She counted them, then looked up and said, "A hundred and ten dollars. Do you suppose that's enough?"

George's mind had been racing, sorting through alternatives, as she found and counted the money. Now he said, "Marnie, I don't know whether it is enough or not, but they won't let Golightly go with you in the plane's cabin. She'd have to go in a crate in the baggage compartment."

Marnie's chin quivered, just once, and then she said firmly, "That won't do at all. We'll just have to walk. I'll stop in the terminal and go to the bathroom and get more water for Golightly. Then we'll be on our way." She stood up and bent to pick up her backpack.

"Wait, wait." George touched her arm. "Listen to me. I've got an idea."

Marnie turned back to him, half hoping. "Look," he said, "I was going to fly today, but no place in particular. I just wanted to get away for awhile. I was going to decide where to go when I got here and filed a flight plan, but I hadn't decided when I got here."

Marnie watched him as he spoke, searching his face, her eyes once more a little wary.

"If you are willing—if you can trust me and want me to help—I'd just as soon fly to Port Angeles as anywhere else, and take you and Golightly with me." Then, suddenly unsure, "Do you want to?" Inside, a part of his mind was yelling at him, "You idiot, what are you getting yourself into? The police may be already looking for her. Stop!" But he ignored it and smiled down at her.

Marnie's mind, too, had been in overdrive. She knew that eight year olds, no matter how smart or responsible, were subject to interference with by almost any officious adult and that her plans were at serious risk as long as she was alone.

Oh, how I wish I were twelve, she thought. But she was a realist and given that her goal was to reach a place of hoped-for safety for Golightly and herself, George's offer was her best option, she thought.

So she said, "Thank you, George. Golightly and I will go with you if you like. There's one thing—do you think Golightly and I can go without being seen by a lot of people? Together we're kind of noticeable."

Since George most fervently did not want to be seen with them, he hastily agreed, and the two of them climbed in the back. He helped Marnie on with her parachute and showed her how it worked. Without being told, Marnie slid way down in the seat and held Golightly firmly as George climbed in, then taxied to the terminal. While he went in and filed his flight plan (without listing any passengers) Marnie kept her head down and Golightly kept her beak shut.

George hurried back out and a few minutes later they were in the air. "We'll be there in thirty minutes—if you need it, there's a relief can in the back—just pull the curtain." Then later, "I'm going to call and reserve a rental car at the airport. We can talk and make plans then, okay?" Marnie nodded and they flew on in silence.

Marnie had never flown before, so far as she knew and the sight of the mountains below them and the clouds and blue sky above was so beautiful that the last knot of fear and worry in her chest loosened a bit. George, meanwhile, paid little attention to the scenery and only minimal attention to his flying, as he tried to work out a plan for the next twenty-four hours.

One problem was Golightly. Fortunately, Marnie seemed able to control her without effort and she stayed quiet with Marnie. He called and was told a car would be waiting for him and his "daughter." Before he'd worked out much more than that, he saw Port Angeles and the airport ahead.

The landing was smooth and they taxied to their designated area near the terminal. He helped Marnie out of her parachute and suggested she slip Golightly inside her jacket, which Marnie quickly did. Golightly clucked once and settled down. They found their car, and George left them in it while he attended to the paperwork and saw his plane hangared for a few days.

George suggested he pick something up at the Safeway deli and that they eat on the beach, which suited Marnie fine. They found an isolated spot on Ediz Hook and ate their bread, cheese, and fruit hungrily. Golightly stayed close to Marnie as the gulls swooped down to investigate.

When they finished, George said, "Marnie, we need to make plans. If it's okay with you, I'd like for the three of us to stay together a few days and maybe I can help you find the 'help' Crystal thought was in the port of angels. We need to find a place to stay, and then we can look around the town and see what we can track down. Okay?"

"What about your job, George?" asked Marnie. "Won't you be in trouble if you don't show up?"

"Oh, I'm on vacation," he replied. "I've got all week. I really didn't have any plans, so nobody will be looking for me."

"Okay then," said Marnie. "What do you think we should do?"

"Well, first I'd like to go to a pet store and get a big cat or dog carrier for Golightly to sleep in, and then we need to find a bed and breakfast that will accept her. Some places won't take pets, you know." *Make that most places,* he thought to himself, but he'd learned long ago that sufficient money could overcome most objections, so he wasn't worried.

Marnie agreed, but pointed out that Golightly would raise a fuss if she were shut in and that they'd have to leave the door open. "She's very smart though—

she goes to the bathroom in the tub or shower and I clean it up with no trouble. That's how she could live in my room."

George was suitably impressed and considerably relieved, as he'd envisioned having to pay for a new carpet when they left the B & B.

They stopped at the Chamber of Commerce on the waterfront, called and found that one of the newer B &B's had two rooms for a week, drove to the pet store and got the carrier and went to a very pleasant Bed and Breakfast. George went in first, and after a five hundred dollar cash deposit for Golightly changed hands, he came back for his "daughter" and her pet.

They were delighted with their rooms and Golightly was shown the bathtub, which she promptly used. After Marnie wiped up, she put out more food and water on the bathroom floor. "We'd better get a newspaper for this," she said.

George made a note of it. His room and bath were across the hall and quite nicely appointed. He suggested they all take a shower and have a short rest or nap before making any more plans.

So for a short time all was quiet. A couple hours later George awoke, listened to the part of his mind that was frantically telling him he'd end up in the penitentiary if he didn't stop now for a minute or two, told it to shut up and went across the hall to knock on Marnie's door. It opened as he raised his hand and a sleepy eyed child looked up at him. He was struck suddenly at how very young she was. Her courage and fortitude ordinarily made her seem much older. Indeed, as the sleepiness left her face and she straightened up, she seemed to gain several years.

For the first time, George looked at her as a person, distinct from the problem she presented, and was surprised at the warmth of real liking he felt. He hadn't realized you could feel friendship for one so young. "Would you like to go sit under those trees and talk a bit?" he asked, gesturing toward some lawn chairs under a clump of trees looking toward the water to the north.

She looked back and saw Golightly roosting comfortably on the arm of a chair, nodded, hung the "do not disturb" sign on her door, and they went outside to their chairs.

Stretched out, watching the ships and boats moving slowly through the Strait, they sat in silence for a while. "I wish I knew what to do next," Marnie finally said.

"Well, Crystal thought of this place as a refuge when things got bad so she must have taken refuge here before, or at least have lived or visited here. Maybe she was raised here, or has a family here. We can check old phone books or city directories tomorrow and see if we can find her name. By the way, what is her last name? Or yours?"

"Smith," said Marnie, somewhat apologetically.

"Oh," said George. "Is that your father's name?" he finally said.

Marnie looked surprised and said, "You know, I never asked. We've always been alone and I never wondered whether or not it was her own name. Maybe it was his. Then we wouldn't know what her name was either, would we?"

"No, but it was a long shot anyway. Look, Marnie, I think our best bet is to spend tomorrow like tourists. Look over the town, chat with people, and try to see what it is about the place that would make it qualify as a refuge. We have no way of knowing whether it was some one or the town itself that meant protection. If the refuge is a place, not a person, maybe we'll run across it. All we can do is try. And let's try to have fun while we do it, okay?" He smiled at the child and she smiled back.

"Done, pardner," she said, in a mock Western accent. They sat a while longer, then decided to go have supper and make an early evening of it.

As they left the house, Marnie asked their host if there was a good place to get vegetarian food. As they headed for the Thai restaurant he recommended, George told himself it figured—anyone who had a chicken for a pet was not likely to eat a chicken, or any animal. He stopped and got a Seattle paper, hoping that news of Marnie's disappearance would not be in it yet. It wasn't, and he felt calmer.

When they went into Thai Peppers, they took a table by the window and looked out at the traffic and passersby as they waited. Finally he looked around the room idly, just to see if their waiter was in sight yet. When his glance got to the corner of the room farthest from the door, his heart almost stopped, or so it felt.

The most beautiful woman he thought he'd ever seen sat perusing her menu. Blonde, slender, perfect features, perfect skin, perfect everything, not more than twenty-five feet from him. And alone. She glanced up, also looking for the waiter, and their glances crossed. George looked away and realized with astonishment and a wry amusement that his hands were trembling.

The waiter came back in the room, hurried over to her and bent, smiling, to take her order. She gave it, then slipped a newspaper out of her bag and disappeared behind it. The waiter disappeared again, returning in a few moments with their meal. George found it hard to concentrate on the food or Marnie, he was so aware of the beautiful stranger behind her paper. Marnie was quiet, too, but it was a companionable meal and they enjoyed it.

Whitney, across the room, wondered why her brief glimpse of the father and his little girl was disturbing her so. There was nothing unusual about them, after all. Both were quite ordinary looking, from the brief glimpse she'd had. The fellow had had a stunned expression when he first saw her, but that had become ordinary to Whitney many years ago.

She risked a glance over the top of her paper just as George bent toward Marnie to hand her the salt shaker. Somehow the mutual protectiveness in the moment when they leaned toward each other tore a hole in her heart and she thought for a moment she would faint. The waiter saw her face and started toward her. "It's all right," she spoke very softly, as she stood. "I'm ill. Forgive me." She turned away and left the room quickly without looking back at the other table again.

When George looked around at the sound of the closing door, she was gone. He didn't know what to do, so he sat with Marnie and they finished their meal. When the waiter came back with the check, he asked, "Is the lady who left okay?" and the waiter said, "Lady say sick. Not eat." George said no more and when they got back in the car Marnie asked, "What lady were you talking about?" George laughed and said, "A real beauty, you couldn't help noticing her. She was there, and then suddenly she wasn't and I just wondered what happened."

When they got back to the house they went to their rooms, Marnie to care for Golightly and then to pull the drapes and go to bed while it was still light out. George did not fare so well, as he tossed and turned and punched his pillow. He wished he had a drink, several drinks, but he needed to be clearheaded tomorrow. He now had a quest of his own, to find that beautiful woman again. He finally fell asleep, to dream of chickens and disappearing women and wilted flowers.

Whitney went right home, where she cried for an hour before she fell asleep. Sometime in the night she woke briefly and knew why the tableau had hurt so badly. It could have been she and Marguerite.

Marnie was awakened the next morning by the same sound she usually was, the low soft clucking of Golightly by her head. She turned and enclosed the beloved form with her arm and whispered into the soft neck feathers, "Dear Golightly, I'm so glad we got away." Then feeling a little disloyal, she explained, "I'm sorry to be worrying Crystal, but we had to leave." She petted her chicken, then mused aloud, "You know, I love Crystal, but I don't miss her at all. Isn't that strange?" Many things are strange in an eight year old's world, so she dismissed the thought, and Crystal, and got ready for the day. She put on her only change of clean clothes and washed the other and hung them in the bathroom. Then she made her way to the dining room where everyone was helping themselves from the sideboard and the hostess was pouring coffee and tea, juice and milk. Marnie loaded up and sat down. It was nice not to fix her own breakfast and everything smelled wonderful.

George came in as Marnie was sitting down, and soon dropped onto the chair beside her. "I need to get some more socks and underwear this morning," she told him. He nodded, mouth full, and then asked their hostess where a good place to get girl's clothes was.

"There are several," she told him. "If you're downtown, try Lamont's." She smiled at Marnie and added, "It's right next door to a really nice gift shop with lots of things kids like—maybe your dad will stop there with you, too." George nodded and asked for more coffee and finally they were done.

"Well, let's get our errands out of the way," said George when they were ready to go an hour later. They parked next to the fountain at the center of downtown and strolled down the brick sidewalks, admiring the overflowing flower baskets and planters at every corner and most stores. "It looks like they're expecting the angels," joked George, as they threaded their way along the busy, tourist-crowded sidewalk. Soon they were at Lamont's, where George told Marnie he'd leave her to do her shopping and meet her in a few minutes at the gift shop next door.

He moved on and stopped to gaze at the window display of kaleidoscopes. He'd always loved them and impulsively decided to get one for Marnie. He opened the door and when a quiet young clerk looked up inquiringly he walked over and said quickly, "My daughter will be here in a minute. Here's my Visa. When we leave wrap up whatever kaleidoscope she favors and I'll be back to get it a little later."

He had barely had time to start looking at them when Marnie came in. "Look, Marnie," he said, handing her one. She took it, looked through the eyepiece and gasped with pleasure. "I've never seen one before," she said, "It's beautiful." They had to look at them all and several other things as well before they left. Marnie enjoyed everything, but expressed no desire for anything. The clerk watched carefully, thinking, *This is something new, a child that isn't, by charm or whine, asking for something.* Her practical eye noticed, though, that as they left Marnie's hand gave a tiny pat to the first kaleidoscope she'd looked at. The clerk wrapped it up, charged it, and handed package and Visa to the nice young father when he dashed in and out about twenty minutes later. The sweetness of the smile he gave her startled her, and when she went back to the office she said to Whitney, "That was a strange kid."

"Umm, what kid?" asked Whitney, looking up from her invoices.

"Little girl with her dad, didn't ask for a thing the whole time she was in here," replied Nora, the clerk. "He'd have given her the moon, too—came back and got that really nice German kaleidoscope we just got in."

"Little girl and her dad?" asked Whitney slowly. "I saw a little girl and her dad last night, and if it was the same two they did seem special. I wonder where the mother is." The bell tinkled as another customer came in, and Nora left to help them. Whitney sat still, feeling vaguely disturbed, then shook her head and went back to her invoices.

Marnie and George went back to the B & B and got Golightly, as Marnie wanted her to have a chance to be outside for a while. She held her pet happily in her lap while they drove out to Lake Crescent and then all three hiked the mile and a half to Marymere Falls. Golightly had a tendency to dawdle, backtrack, pursue sundry bugs, and stare vacantly at ferns along the trail, evidently puzzled as to their identity or purpose. Marnie was perfectly content to indulge her and then uncomplainingly carried her when she decided to rest awhile.

George had found it really strange that anyone could be attracted to a chicken, for Heaven's sake, but as he watched Golightly's head lean trustingly on Marnie's chest and her eyes close in contentment as Marnie sturdily marched along the trail, he felt a stirring of affection for the bird himself. *I must be crazy,* he thought, and asked if Marnie would like him to carry Golightly for a while. "No, thank you," she said. "She's not heavy and she's used to me."

They spent a pleasant afternoon and George stopped to get a paper as they came back through town. *Time to face reality,* he thought, as he paged through it. Nothing. He looked again, slowly and carefully, even the tiny items this time. Nothing. He was angry and relieved both, as he wondered if, by some chance, Crystal and Rick hadn't reported her missing.

They drove back to the B & B, but before they got out of the car he turned and asked, "Marnie, do you think it's possible Crystal hasn't reported you missing?"

Marnie didn't look at him when she answered, but there was a tiny tinge of sadness in her voice when she said quietly, "I was counting on it when I left. I knew if she did I'd be easy to spot and get caught right away." She drew a deep breath and looked at him then. "You'd have to know Crystal to understand. She's trusting and soft, not like most grown-ups. She believes what Rick tells her, or anyone does. He'll say he's sure I've run off to be with some wonderful family that I've met somehow. She'll think I have, but will want to get in touch with me. Rick will say 'Leave her alone, ungrateful kid. She doesn't care about us.' And she'll cry and say she misses me, but she'll give in. She's not a strong person."

"That makes it easier for us, and gives us more time, but I'm sorry, Marnie."

"Don't be, George. She loves me, but she loves him more, right now," and Marnie opened the door and carried Golightly inside. George followed, gift store sack in hand. When they reached their rooms, George handed her the sack and said, "Here's something to remember our day by. Why don't we go out to supper in an hour or so, okay?"

Encumbered by chicken and shopping bags, she got the door open, nodded okay, and went inside. She let the sacks drop onto the carpet, sat on the edge of the bed, and let her tears fall silently on Golightly's feathers, not for the first time.

She'd counted on Crystal's not calling the police, but it hurt all the same. Crystal did love her, she knew she did! It's just that there wasn't much to Crystal, or her love. Marnie hated to think the words, but she knew they were true, and her heart ached for something more.

"Don't be a baby," she told herself, and got up and blew her nose and wiped her eyes, then fed and watered Golightly, put her in the bathtub and cleaned up after her. Only then did she open her packages of socks and panties and put them away. Last, she opened the package from George and whispered, "Oh no, oh how lovely," when she saw the kaleidoscope. She slipped off her shoes, lay on the bed and looked toward the window. For a half hour she lay there, watching the gorgeous colors and shapes form and reform in never-ending variety. The pain in her sore child's heart eased and she gave herself over to pure joy of beauty beyond sorrow.

It was a more cheerful child who accompanied George to supper this night, and she thanked him shyly for his gift. "I've loved them all my life," he said. "I must have a dozen at least, every one I've ever gotten. I'll show them to you sometime. Now, where would you like to eat tonight?"

"I liked that Thai place; did you? I'd like to try their vegetables with green curry next time," Marnie said. George hadn't realized how much he'd hoped she'd say that and he felt quite elated going in. But they were early and the place was half empty yet. No beautiful woman anywhere.

You idiot, he told himself. *She was probably a tourist and is five hundred miles from here tonight.* No sooner had he thought this than she came in. She didn't see them; in fact she seemed abstracted as she sat down facing George and picked up the menu. The waiter hurried over and she looked up and smiled and said, "The usual, Lin." He nodded and hurried away.

She must be a regular, George thought, and bent to study his own menu. "I think I'll have the green curry, too, Marnie." Then he stopped, for Marnie had an odd look on her face.

She was looking straight ahead, almost as if she were trying to see something that wasn't there. She shook herself slightly and said, "I'm sorry, what did you say George?"

"Marnie, what's wrong?" he asked.

"I don't know," she said in a bewildered voice. "I heard a voice just now, somebody talking to a waiter, and I had the weirdest feeling. I can't explain it, but I wanted to run to it. It was like a beacon, only calling me." She shook herself and looked down at her clenched hands.

Whitney looked over, to see George kneeling by Marnie's chair, holding both her hands. Then she flung herself against him, arms around him, crying soundlessly. George picked her up and carried her out, still crying, and her arms around his neck. As they went through the door Marnie opened her eyes and looked past Whitney, seeing nothing. Whitney sat paralyzed as they got into a parked car and drove away.

"Lindsay," she thought. "Lindsay Campbell's eyes." She closed her eyes and saw his face in front of her, eyes filled with tears as he told her how sorry he was nine years ago. She had just told him she was pregnant as a result of their slightly tipsy encounter at the faculty Christmas party where they had both begun teaching in September. She had not blamed him, but felt he should know. But he blamed himself, and with a wife and three children already, there was nothing he could do about it, not even offer to pay for an abortion. It was the last time she had seen him, as she had resigned immediately, and he left at the end of the school year.

Marguerite was born that summer, and although Whitney did not need to work, thanks to Great Grandmother Barnes, she did have occasional times when she needed someone reliable to care for Marguerite. Diane had impressed Whitney with her sweet disposition and gentle ways with the baby. So when she came to Whitney one day in tears because her apartment had been sold and she couldn't find another one, Whitney asked if she wanted to be a full-time nanny. Diane was ecstatic, and she grew to love baby Marguerite. And so it went for some three years, with a happy, beautiful child the center of two women's lives. Then one afternoon Whitney came home, happy and excited about a new program her alumni group had put together for helping fund a children's summer music camp. The instant she'd opened the door she knew the house was empty. She had never seen Diane or Marguerite again.

Her mind refused to revisit the hours, the days, and the months after she opened the door until finally the case was off the TV news and the newspapers and the tongues of everyone she knew. Then she started the long, lonely hunt she now thought she'd be on the rest of her life.

Dazed, she ate her food mechanically, tasting nothing, while her memory ground on and finally came to a halt with tonight. She wondered vaguely why that child with Lindsay's eyes was crying.

Her fork clattered from her hand and she felt as if her blood had turned to ice. Marguerite? Could she be Marguerite? Frantically her mind tried to remember the girl—how old was she? What did she look like? Who was her father? Where were they? She flung money down by her plate and raced out, leaving Lin standing staring after her.

At home, she held the phone in shaking hands. When she heard Nora's calm voice she tried to get hold of herself, but her voice was unsteady when she said, "Nora, do you remember the man and the little girl in the store this morning? How old was she?"

"Almost nine, maybe 10, I'd say," replied Nora. "Or maybe not quite that. She had been around grown-ups a lot, I'd say, and it's hard to tell with kids like that. They usually act older than they are. Why? What about her?"

"I'll explain later. It's important. Did either one say anything about their plans or where they are staying, or are they local?"

"Gee, Whitney, I didn't pay that much attention. I know they seemed close, and I assumed he was her father, though she called him George. Wait, I remember now, he said "my daughter" will be here in a few minutes and gave me his Visa to charge that kaleidoscope for her. I don't remember his last name, but it would be on our copy of his charge. I think he called her Marnie."

"Thanks, Nora. I'll see you tomorrow," said Whitney. "I won't be in in the morning though, so look after things, will you?" As soon as she hung up, Whitney grabbed her purse and sweater and drove carefully to the shop. It was still light out of course, and a few diners, movie patrons, and teenagers were still on the street as she let herself into the shop. Her hands shook as she went through the charge card slips for the day. At last she looked down at the one in her hand, for a kaleidoscope charged to George Morgan, 147 Park Town Place, Seattle. She wondered if he was Glenda Morgan's son. If so, he wasn't married—there'd been a divorce not too long ago, if she remembered correctly, and no children.

Whoever's George he was, where was he? They must still be in town. No one would take a child that age home to Seattle at this hour of the night. Unless she was ill! The thought panicked Whitney. They must be in a bed and breakfast, as they didn't look like motel people and there was no hotel in Port Angeles.

She pulled the phone book over, found Bed & Breakfasts, and started down the list, calling each one. "Hello, this is Whitney Fairfield. I'm trying to reach a customer, George Morgan. Are he and his daughter staying with you?" The third call was success.

"Yes, Mr. Morgan and his daughter are with us, but they are out for dinner right now, would you like to leave a message?"

"Yes, please. Would you tell Mr. Morgan that he was inadvertently over-charged for a gift he bought his daughter at my shop today? I'd like to refund that amount to him. Would you ask him to call me when he gets in?" and she gave her number. Then she sat back and stared out the window, her mind a jumble of memories and speculations, her hands knotted in her lap.

Marnie had stopped crying before they got back to the bed and breakfast, though she was still hiccupping when they parked. He came around to pick her up again, but she tried to smile and said softly, "I'm okay, George. I'm sorry. I don't know what happened or why I got so upset. I won't do it anymore."

"It's all right, honey," he said gently, and his heart hurt for her. They walked to their rooms and Golightly fluttered and rustled over to meet her. "Oh Golightly," she said, "It's past suppertime for you," and picked up her chicken and held her close. One tear fell on the shining feathers, and then she briskly set about caring for her—food, water, bathtub.

George watched a minute and then said, "Why don't you go on to bed, Marnie? We've had a long day. Knock on my door if you need me, okay?" She nodded and he walked across the hall. There was a note on his door, "Please call Mrs. Fairfield at 452-2130. Important." He glanced at his watch—only 9:00. Then went in and dialed.

When the phone rang, Whitney took a deep breath and then said, "Hello, this is Whitney Fairfield."

A nice masculine voice said, "You asked me to call?"

"Oh yes, Mr. Morgan," she replied, "you were in my shop this morning and we inadvertently overcharged you quite a bit for that lovely kaleidoscope for your daughter. I'm going to be gone tomorrow and wondered if I might bring your refund to you this evening, on my way to an engagement."

George was quite taken with her voice, firm, but low and musical, and he didn't stop to wonder where she'd be going at that hour of the night, though it was still light, or why her clerk couldn't give the refund to him if he'd stop in tomorrow. "Of course," he replied. "You know where the B & B is don't you?" At her assent, he said, "I was just going out to unwind under the trees to the side of the place, where you can sit and watch the lights come on. I'll watch for you."

A few moments later a car pulled up in front and she came toward him over the grass. George sat up in astonishment. It was that beautiful woman who'd rushed out of the restaurant. Without realizing it, he gave her the full force of his smile—the smile that was famous among his friends and family. She paused a second, then came on, her hand outstretched.

"Mr. Morgan?" Her voice was softer than on the phone, but she seemed a little tense to him.

"Oh yes, Miss Fairfield? Sit down, won't you?" and he indicated a chair.

She dropped into it with a sigh. "All right, just for a moment. I've had an exhausting day and these chairs are wonderfully comfortable, aren't they?"

When George had seated himself across from her, she slipped her hand into her bag and handed him an envelope. "I'm so sorry for the mistake. Nora, my clerk, didn't realize that we got this last shipment of kaleidoscopes at a special rate, and she marked them with our old, usual price."

He laid the envelope on the table and replied, "It's good of you to track me down. The price seemed reasonable to me—I've looked at many of them over the years and Marnie is enjoying it enormously."

"Marnie?" she asked. "That's a lovely name. Is it a nickname?"

George started to reply, "I haven't any idea," caught himself in time, and said a little hurriedly, "You could say so," and sought to turn the conversation to less risky ground. But Whitney had caught the hesitation and her heart began to pound.

"Nora was quite taken with Marnie and she said she had lovely manners for such a young girl. How old is Marnie?" George knew the answer to this one, and he answered confidently, "She's eight, but she does seem older."

"Why, I have a daughter who's eight," Whitney exclaimed. "When is your little girl's birthday?" A peculiar note of pain in her voice caught his ear, but his brain was frantically trying to decide whether to admit he didn't know, or give a date out of the blue. He was about to blurt out something, he had no idea what, when he saw, over his shoulder, Marnie open the door and come toward them across the grass.

"Here's Marnie now, you can meet her yourself," he said with some relief, as he rose to meet Marnie. Something in Whitney's frozen stillness caught his attention and when he glanced down he saw that her eyes were closed and her face was pale. Her hands were knotted hard in her lap.

"Are you okay?" he asked anxiously, his attention on her.

She whispered, "Yes."

He turned as Marnie came on up. "Are you feeling better, honey?" he asked, smiling at her.

"Oh yes," she said, "but I didn't want to be alone right now and I saw you out here. So I came along." She looked inquiringly toward Whitney, who sat still with her back to her and he said, "Marnie, I'd like you to meet Miss Fairfield, who stopped by with a refund for me. She's the lady who owns that great shop where we got your kaleidoscope this morning."

As Whitney turned to face Marnie, a last shaft of sunlight lit up her beautiful face and made the tears blurring her eyes sparkle.

Marnie's hand clutched his with a grip of iron, but her voice was the choked voice of a three year old when she said, "Mama? Mama?" then flung herself at Whitney, crying, "Who are you? Who are you?"

Whitney had dropped to her knees and held out her arms at that first "Mama" and she held Marnie so tightly she could hardly breathe, laughing and crying and whispering over and over "Marguerite, Marguerite." Marnie's hair was wet with her tears. Marnie was crying, too, and poor George stood over them, feeling completely bewildered and helpless.

At last Marnie pulled back a little and said, "But I don't understand. I don't know you—and yet I do somehow. You're in my dreams sometimes and now you're real. Crystal is my mother and yet I called you 'Mama.'" Then she looked up at George and said helplessly, "I don't understand, George."

He lifted Marnie to her feet and eased her into a chair, then offered his hand to the disheveled Whitney and got her seated next to Marnie, noting that their hands both reached for the other's and clasped firmly. He pulled up his own chair opposite the two, and said, "Now let's see if we can get to the bottom of this. You first, Whitney."

So there in the gathering darkness, Whitney told of Marnie's birth, the coming of her nanny, Diane, the three happy years in the big old house and the disappearance of Marguerite and Diane. The police, the publicity, the search by public and then private detectives, the end of the trail in Port Angeles, and Whitney's long search and waiting since then.

Marnie began with her memories of early moves with Crystal, her mother, the jobs, the boyfriends, and at the last, Rick and his threat to Golightly, her flight from home, meeting George and their search for a refuge for Marnie at "the port of the angels."

Marnie repeated Crystal's "if things get too bad we can always go back to Miz Rich or the port of the angels." Whitney said that Diane used to joke sometimes and call her "Miz Rich" and that the detectives had found that Diane and her mother had lived in Port Angeles at one time.

"Didn't you realize the enormous risk you were taking in order to help Marnie?" Whitney asked at last, as they all sat quietly under the trees.

"Yes, I did," replied George, "but I never felt I had a choice. Marnie needed help and there was no one else. Then pretty soon I loved them both, and I quit even thinking about it. But now," he said, getting up, "we'd better get to bed. We can make plans tomorrow, when we've adjusted a bit." He looked at their linked hands. "I'll tell our host there will be one more in Marnie's room tonight—it's a big bed—and that we'll be leaving tomorrow."

He stayed with them only long enough to see Whitney meet with Golightly's approval, then saw the host and paid him before going back to his own room. In bed, he looked at the ceiling before falling asleep and whispered "thank you."

The next morning they left before breakfast, going first to the shop where they picked up several things for Marnie and then to Whitney's small but beautiful house. From a closet in the second bedroom, now Marnie's, she brought out a sealed cardboard carton, that when opened, proved to contain all of three year old Marguerite's toys that were left behind. George felt tears sting the back of his eyes when Marnie reached for and then hugged a somewhat worn bear, and whispered "Teddy, it's you, isn't it?" Whitney quite frankly kept bursting into tears and then saying, "Don't mind me, I'm sorry," and wiping her eyes.

They all went in the kitchen, finally, and Whitney fixed them fruit and toast and coffee. She poured soy milk for Marnie, saying, "I'm sorry I don't have regular milk, but I'm a vegetarian." Marnie looked up with relief and said, "That's okay, so am I." George heard himself saying, "And so am I," and knew that it was true. What else could he be, when his future wife and daughter were?

And as he looked around the kitchen with the sun shining on the water seen from the kitchen window, the three people around the table, Golightly roosting on an arm of the fourth chair near the window and clucking softly now and then, he knew that he was home at last. The gratitude and dawning awareness of him as an attractive man that lit Whitney's eyes when she spoke to him assured him it wouldn't be long. Maybe they would even stay here—he remembered Whitney's quoting Diane that Port Angeles was a good place to raise a family—in this little house flooded now with happiness.

George got up and went to the sink for more water. He stood a minute, looking out over the Strait, whispered "thank you" again and turned back to the three who mattered more than everything in the world to him. He realized he'd only known them three days, and smiled. It didn't matter. He would know them always, now.

Ann Gilson is a retired university librarian who has been active in animal rescue for more than sixty years. Her twin passions are books and cats, and she cares for a large collection of each.

MEET THE JUDGES

FINDERS KEEPERS

By Erika Hamerquist

A Coming of Age Novella

Lowell Johnson was busy putting the finishing touches on his suicide when the cat came along and gave him something to live for.

Plan and Cat occurred nearly in the same moment. He was sitting at the kitchen table, his old .22 Winchester lying dismantled on a mat of old *Gazettes*, the gun oil sweet in his nostrils, rag in hand, when suddenly it all came together. See, the mess had been the only loose end left. He'd known for years he wanted to die, and all the estate rigmarole was taken care of; the means was ready to hand—hell, he had a whole cabinet full of means—but the one thing, the only thing, that had stopped him was the mess. Someone would have to come across his body, and he knew for a fact a thing like that could spoil a person's day, maybe even the rest of a lifetime. Lowell didn't want that. Especially since the person was likely to be his daughter Gayle. She had a habit of checking up on him every other day or so, ingrained over the seven years since Virgie died. Or it might be his friend Jack. Jack had been showing up unannounced with increasing frequency, trying to get Lowell interested in one wild scheme after another. Last one, a road trip up the Al-Can.

So there he was, stuck on the problem of how to arrange it so some hardened professional would be the one to find his remains. Someone who'd collect the moment as a war story to impress friends instead of one of those post-distressful traumas the psychiatrists were always going on about. Gayle was tough, but not *that* tough. And Jack? Well, the thing of it was, Lowell was worried about lowering himself in his friend's esteem. He could see Jack sauntering in, that obnoxious whistle twittering into silence, and after the shock wore off saying something like, "Damn, Lowell. I thought you were better than this." Lowell didn't believe in the afterlife and was pretty sure he wouldn't be around to hear those words, but he didn't much like the image of his corpse receiving a lecture while it lay there all defenseless.

One obvious solution was to do away with himself in a remote corner of the woods somewhere. But then *any* poor slob might stumble across him. College kids on a hike. Tourists. DNR employees. Besides, there was hardly anything that counted as remote on the Olympic Peninsula anymore.

Another idea had been to call 911 and *tell* them he was going to do it, then they'd have somebody on the way lickety-split to bag him up. Problem was, they might try to talk him out of it while they had him on the phone. He'd have to hang up in some dispatcher's face, and he'd always had a problem with that. Hours of his evenings had been spent listening to telephone marketers pitching their wares 'cause he couldn't muster what he considered the plain rudeness to cut them off. Hanging up on someone would be harder, he figured, than squeezing the trigger. Also, there was the chance 911 would get someone out to his place before he managed to pull it off. Then he'd end up locked in the loony-bin, with strangers talking like they knew him personally, and if he ever got out they'd be watching him like a hawk. Especially Gayle.

But that night, sitting there at the dinette cleaning his gun, it came to him: What he needed to do was very calmly call the sheriff's office to report a crime. Something minor, but big enough that they'd feel obligated to check it out right away. He could say he'd come home from the Safeway store to find his door broken in and a bunch of guns stolen. That should get 'em out. He'd leave the front door propped open, then do the deed like he'd arranged, with the note safety-pinned to his chest, the doubled-over tarp underneath him and the towel draped over his head. In the kitchen, 'cause any blood that leaked out would be easier to clean up off the linoleum. Gayle would get the house, so he wanted to be sure and leave it nice and neat in case she decided to sell the mobile and move back into the place she grew up in. Presumably the deputy wouldn't do anything so stupid as call her and have her come over and identify him. That would ruin everything. Okay, so he would add a P.S. "Please don't allow my family or friends to view me in this condition."

Lowell was getting up to go get the note from its hiding place when he heard the crash, and in that instant he wondered, *Will I hear it? Will it be as loud as that?* Then the circle of his wondering swelled beyond his current obsession, and he thought, *What the hell?!*

The sound had come from out on the back porch. He went to the door, flipped the light switch and stared out the window into a confetti of moths and gnats dancing in the sudden limelight against a backdrop as black as tar.

The cat was crouched on the porch railing, a gray tom which would've been big as a coon if it hadn't been so skinny. Jowly as Louis Armstrong, ears tattered, eyes gold-green orbs, it stared at Lowell as if it'd been waiting for him there for years.

On the floorboards beneath the cat lay shards of ceramic and a chunk of potting soil, mummified into permanent pot-shape by bound roots. That potting soil had been tamped into that flowerpot by Virgie's own hand. Never mind that the plant—and Lowell couldn't remember what kind it'd been—had withered away years ago. That flowerpot had stood on the porch railing for a good part of his marriage, and now it was gone. Like Virgie.

His first instinct was to dive for his .22, but there it was in pieces on the table. "God *damn* it!" he howled, hating the querulous squeal in his aging voice. He lunged for the door and jerked it open, bent on barehanded revenge.

The cat dropped from the rail with a surprisingly solid thud, streaked down the steps and off toward the machine shed. Lowell followed with a lot less fluidity. By the time he reached the shed, jarred and winded, he knew it was hopeless. He turned on the light anyway and peered into the cobwebbed corners, trying hard not to see the truck even though it was right there, big as a pink elephant, hood still up.

No sign of the cat, though.

Still trying not to see the truck Lowell turned off the light and trudged back to the house. Mounting the porch stairs he felt like he had a whiskey hangover, not that he'd experienced many. He dropped to his knees next to the broken pot—something he realized, too late, he was too old to do. He should've lowered himself in easy stages or not at all.

"Oh, Virgie," he groaned, and felt a febrile wave of impotent rage and all-too-potent grief roll over him. His heart raced; his flesh went from hot to cold, and he was terrified it was about to happen again. No! No, he wanted to *kill* himself, not *die*! No, that wasn't putting it right: He wanted to make sure he *did* die. None of those half measures. No lingering on, no drool, no wheelchairs, no attendants and incontinence for Lowell Samuel Johnson!

It took a minute, but he pulled himself together. It took somewhat longer to pull himself back to his feet, but he achieved that too, then gathered the largest pieces of the pot. Mexico. Guadalajara. That's where they'd picked it up. Fifth anniversary. Their honeymoon had been at Sol Duc Hot Springs; there hadn't been the money to travel then. Actually, there hadn't been the money five years later, either, but they'd done it anyhow. His idea. Virgie was always the practical one. Always said why should they go anywhere when Sequim was already the most beautiful place on the planet? All she needed was her garden to feel herself in heaven on earth. "And you, Lowell, dear. I couldn't do without the serpent in my Eden, keeping me warm in his coils every night."

He set the pieces on the railing where the pot had stood. He hadn't the heart to carry them into the house. He could see there was no hope of gluing them back together. Besides, the damage was done. The integrity of the illusion was shattered even more surely than the ceramic. He might cobble it back together but he'd never again be able to glance at it in passing and think, *Virgie's here because that's still there.* He was losing her in bits and pieces everywhere he turned. Used to be he could look out at the flowerbeds and think, *Virgie's here because that's still there.* Now he didn't have the strength or willpower to keep up with the yard work, and was damned if he'd call anyone in to do it. The annual beds and vegetable garden had been the first to disappear, then the perennials had run wild and started dying off. The shrubbery and berry vines were descending into chaos too. Next would be the ornamental trees ... the orchard. Virgie's heaven was disappearing year by year, and he was standing by, afraid to save it and afraid to see it go. One of the many ways he'd failed her. One of the many reasons for the plan.

Another was the truck. Dry-mouthed, Lowell stared across the yard at the angular hulk of the machine shed. For all his determination not to see the truck when it was right before his eyes, of course he *had* seen it, and was still seeing it now in his mind. For two days it had been all he could think about, inspiring him to revisit the details of his suicide over the somehow soothing exercise of cleaning his gun collection.

Day before yesterday he'd decided to change the oil in his old Chev, even though it didn't need it, at the rate he put on miles. Despite having been an auto mechanic for over fifty years he still got the occasional yen to get his hands greasy.

At first all had gone well. He'd let the engine run a bit to warm the oil, then shut down, lifted the hood, changed the air filter—all like he'd done a hundred thousand times. It was after he slid under the truck on his little padded trolley that things went to hell. He'd been pleased with himself that he'd gotten down there on his back with no trouble, since lately this was an iffy maneuver, but satisfaction fled when he couldn't get the old oil filter loose. The plug on the oil pan had come out fine and he'd already drained that off into a rubber tub. The new filter with its delicate smear of oil round the gasket was ready to go, but no matter how he gripped and twisted on the old one it resisted as stubbornly as if someone had soldered it on. Since he was the one who'd put it there he knew for a fact he wouldn't have over tightened it. A strap wrench would've done the trick, but that meant rolling out, getting up to grab one, then getting back down again. A mere inconvenience twenty years ago; now something to be avoided at all costs. So he'd gone at it again, grabbing the filter like the throat of his worst enemy, cursing like ten sailors. And then …

He didn't know what, then. He'd roused from nothingness into profound discomfort. Above him hung a viper's nest of steel, cast aluminum and black rubber. For a long, long moment he'd had no conception of what he was looking at … who he was … anything. Knew only that he ached everywhere that hadn't gone numb, and that he'd wet himself.

It had taken him a good five minutes of agony and weeping frustration to wriggle out from under the truck. Now, standing on the porch with the night breeze buffeting his clammy skin, he shuddered to think of what might've been. What *had* been was bad enough. He'd wet himself, for Christ's sake! If Gayle or Jack had dropped by and found him in that predicament the humiliation, alone, should've been sufficient to kill him! But not fast enough. Not as fast as a bullet to the head. Death was fine; suffering, whether of the body or the spirit, Lowell would just as soon do without. That was the point of all his arrangements.

He was all right now, though, he told himself firmly. The fateful pants were in the trash, too tainted to be recovered by a washing. True, the oil change was still only half done but in a day or two he'd get under there with a strap wrench and take care of it. In the meantime, he couldn't bring himself to touch the truck, not even to close the hood.

"Damn cat!" he said out loud, to distract himself. Then he went back into the house to put the .22 back together and load it. Next time, he'd be ready.

*   *   *   *

He was eating a bowl of granola and slightly soured milk the next morning when he was startled by a rap on the back door window. His daughter Gayle stood outside. She wasn't the kind to come in without an invitation. Very respectful of people's "space," was Gayle. He waved her in, thinking unhappily that a year ago he would've heard her steps on the stairs if not her car in the drive.

"Hi, Dad," she said, shutting the door behind her. She didn't sit down, but studied him through her glasses as if she were doing a twenty-point check. A beautiful strong-boned girl once, she was rather plain in middle-age but seemed content with herself and her looks, which Lowell found both restful and rare in a woman. "I was going to do some grocery shopping and thought I'd stop by to see if you need anything."

Lowell told her he could use a half-gallon of milk and got up to get his wallet. She didn't offer to pay for it for him. They'd stopped having that argument long ago.

"What happened to the planter?" she asked, giving a nod toward the porch. "Wind?"

The wind in the Sequim valley was capable of many iniquities. Lowell wished he'd disposed of the shards before Gayle saw them, but then again she likely would've noticed the pot missing anyhow. He shook his head. "Damn stray cat got up there and knocked it off."

"That's a shame." She eyed his breakfast. "Dad, man does not live by granola alone. Why not scramble an egg now and then? How about if I pick you up some bacon, too?"

Lowell peeled another bill off the fold in his wallet. He had no intention of scrambling any eggs—he hadn't had an appetite in years, so why bother cooking?—but said, "That'd be fine."

He followed her out onto the porch, and winced when he saw her lens-magnified eyes rove toward the machine shed. From this angle the front grill of the pickup was visible, and the fact that the hood was up.

"Truck break down?" she asked.

"No. Just changing the oil."

"Hmm." She eyed him, then reached out and laid a hand on the pieces of broken flower pot. "Mom had this forever. It's really too bad."

"Cat sticks around here, I'm gonna shoot it," Lowell volunteered, realizing too late that it was an unwise impulse.

Gayle's eyes got bigger and her mouth smaller, sure signs of disapproval. She hated guns on both general and very specific principles. "You can't do that, Dad."

Lowell wasn't in the mood for dissembling. He'd slept hardly at all, fixated on the cat, and woken up madder than he'd gone to bed. "Why the hell not?" he demanded truculently.

"For one thing, the neighbors. You've got folks too close by for you to be firing a gun around here."

Lowell glowered past the three hundred feet of increasingly wild yard down to his southern boundary. At one time all the land beyond had been alfalfa and dairy pasture, with the mountains as a backdrop. Now it was pimpled with pastel-colored cookie-cutter houses, a new one every time he turned around, it seemed.

Gayle wasn't through. "For another, I believe there's a law against shooting stray animals. It might be somebody's lost pet."

Lowell snorted. "When I was a kid if there were too many cats in the barn Dad'd toss 'em all in a gunny sack and spray it with buckshot till it quit moving."

Gayle gave him a look that said she was wondering if maybe that was the root of all his problems. "You wouldn't get away with that kind of thing these days," she said. "Thank God. Look. I'm going to pick you up a couple cans of cat food—"

"What! You expect me to *feed* that mangy—! No, sir!"

"Let me finish. There's a group called Peninsula Friends of Animals here in town. They help people trap feral cats and—"

"And take 'em to the pound to be gassed? How's that any better than a nice quick bullet in the head?" It was the kind of question Lowell had been weighing a lot, these days.

"They don't take them to the pound, Dad. They get them fixed up by a volunteer vet then bring them back—"

"No. I don't want that fleabag on my place. Sooner shoot it."

"Dad. We'll trap the cat, get it fixed and healthy, then *I'll* take it. That is, if we find out it doesn't belong to anybody already. We'll check that out first. Did it look thin?"

"Rack of bones."

She shook her head. "Poor thing. It's probably lost and going begging from porch to porch. I'll bring you back some cat food. You can start putting a little out every night so it gets used to being fed. That way it'll be easier to trap. I'll arrange to get the trap out here Monday, if I can."

"What if it never comes back?"

"Then your worries are over. Your goal is to make it go away, isn't it?"

His goal was to make it dead, but he decided not to say so.

✳   ✳   ✳   ✳

An hour later Gayle was back with the groceries. He hadn't done anything since she'd left but wash his bowl and spoon and stare into space. "I picked up your mail," she said. "It doesn't look like you checked the box the last couple days."

Lowell admitted he hadn't.

Watching his daughter set three cans of cat food on his counter he mused that he had no complaints there. When Virgie first got sick, Gayle had quit her teaching job in Seattle and moved out here to help look after her. Hadn't moved into the house—she would've considered that imposing no matter what he and Virgie said. No, she'd bought herself a dumpy mobile on an acre lot over in Carlsborg. Had it fixed up pretty nice now, with a little garden. Said she didn't regret leaving the city, even though her jobs these days were hit and miss and barely got her by. Her and the kid. Xavier. Now who the hell named their child something that began with an X? Probably she'd been thinking of that black fella, the one in the suit and hornrims she'd had a poster of in her room back when she was going to college.

To Lowell, the kid was an enigma. He couldn't recall ever having had a conversation with him, but then he'd never started one. Neither had the kid. Maybe they were equally to blame? No. The boy'd been but six years old when Gayle brought him out here to live. Lowell knew he should've taken him in hand, played the grandpa. But Virgie'd been so sick ... And now? Well hell. Lowell just plain didn't know what to say to a teenager these days. And what was the point anyhow? He didn't plan on being around much longer.

As if reading his mind, Gayle turned away from the fridge where she'd stowed milk, eggs, bacon and a carton of orange juice Lowell hadn't ordered and said, "I've been thinking: Why don't you let me bring Xav over to help out with that oil change? He'd love to work on a car with you. He's excited about learning how, for when he gets one of his own."

Lowell couldn't picture that slouching close-mouthed kid excited about *any-thing*, let alone telling his mother so. "What could I teach that boy about engines?" he growled, with an irrational swell of annoyance. "He doesn't even know how to pick out a pair of pants! Buys 'em so big they hang round his knees so he can't take a step without hitchin' 'em up!"

"That's called sagging, Dad. It's meant to show solidarity with the brothers in prison who aren't allowed to wear belts."

"Well, what I want to know then is what the hell does that boy want to be doin' *showin' solidarity* with anyone in prison for?"

"It's the style. All the kids do it these days."

"They're all damn fools, then. As I suspected all along."

Gayle grinned. "Like your grandparents suspected of your generation, no doubt." Then her smile slipped off and she added, "He's a good kid, Dad."

Lowell didn't say anything. Just sat staring at the cans of cat food, chewing the insides of his cheeks.

After Gayle had gone he began to worry in earnest. Now that she knew about the oil change he'd actually have to get it done. Crawl under there again, confront his nemesis. He'd give it one try with a strap wrench; if that didn't work he'd leave the old filter on, get the plug back in, toss in the fresh quarts and call it good.

Eventually he got up, went out onto the porch, picked up the broken flower-pot and started down the stairs with it toward the garbage can. On the way he had second thoughts and carried the shards out to his property line and set them on top of a fence post. He couldn't put a piece of Virgie in the trash. Someone else could come along and do it after he was gone.

When he turned back, a car was pulling into his turn-around, a well-preserved Seventy-something Cutlass. The tires had barely stopped rolling before a well-preserved seventy-something Jack Horton hopped neatly out of it, already whistling and looking suspiciously go-to-meetin' in dark brown slacks and pale blue shirt. "Lowell!" he bellowed. He had an obscene head of hair for a man his age, glossy white and standing tall as the fluff on top of a Denny's coconut creme pie. "Ready to go?"

"Where the hell you think I'm going?" Lowell retorted. He'd learned long ago to show no sign of flimsiness where Jack was concerned unless he was in the mood to be taken up by the tornado. Jack was a man of a thousand plans, and if he had his way Lowell would be playing sidekick in every one of them. For the first fifty years that had been fine with Lowell, but lately, especially since Virgie died, Jack's roping-in had taken on an evangelical quality Lowell would just as soon do without. Jack was Lowell's last living friend. They'd quite literally known each other all their lives, having been born a month apart in the same hospital to mothers who were best friends and fathers who raised and milked cows on neigh-boring farms. Now Jack was trying to orchestrate Lowell's "golden years" into something other than the tarnished wasteland Lowell perceived.

"Hold on. Don't tell me you forgot?" Jack exclaimed, swinging the car door shut with a flourish. He was the flourishing type. "You said you'd come with me to the center today."

Lowell noticed how he left off the word "senior" before "center." If he hadn't known about the omission he might've felt a tickle of intrigue. "Center" has such a ring of vibrant centrality. "Center of attention," "center of the universe," "com-mand center." But stick the word "senior" back in and what did you have? Train-ing ground for the nursing home. "I said I'd think about it," Lowell said. But he hadn't. It was unthinkable. "I would've called if I'd decided to go."

For all his hail-fellow-well-met buffoonery, Jack was no idiot. "And I'd've brought an extra set of skates for the devil," he said, grinning, "'Cause hell would've been froze over. C'mon, Lowell. That's why I came over so early. Figured I'd need to provide a little face-to-face encouragement."

Lowell shut his eyes and clenched his jaw, seeing feline vandals and urine stains. How much more could a man stand? "Don't," he strained through his teeth, which were all still his own unlike Jack's store-bought set.

"How 'bout some coffee?" Jack said. "Or are you about to chase me outa here with one o' your shotguns?"

Jack wasn't a sitter. He roved the house while Lowell got the coffee going, giving himself the excuse to shout so Lowell could hear him from whichever corner he happened to be poking into. It seemed like Jack was always exercising something, be it legs, lungs, or his sense of humor. Lowell couldn't understand how Jack had kept hold of that—his sense of humor, that is. His own had dried up and blown away ages ago. Maybe he'd never really *had* one. Maybe Jack had been the humor-bearer for the both of them through childhood and youth, right up until Virgie took over the job. Lowell had vague recollections of finding things amusing once … laughing … but it all seemed so unlikely now. Still, it was strange that Jack could find humor anywhere after the life he'd led. He'd been the one who had trouble holding down a job, flitting from log camps to Alaska canneries to paper mills to road crews. He'd been the one to marry a harpy from Forks who later dragged him through a divorce that divided Clallam County down the middle before the fur stopped flying. He was the one whose only child, a son, went bad and died in a shootout with a passel of cops in downtown Tacoma. He was the one who survived alcoholism and a cancer scare—even spent some time in jail. But look at him now! The Twelve-Step poster boy. The door-to-door solicitor for new memberships to the local seniors club. The man who was either whistling or laughing or cracking a joke like a raw egg over some fool straight-man sidekick's head.

"You know the problem with you?" Jack said, wandering back into the kitchen. "You've lost count of your blessings."

Lowell covertly rolled his eyes as he poured out two mugs of acid-strong black brew.

"Another problem with you is you can't face the fact you ain't twenty-five any more." Jack paused in front of the porch window, which gave him the same view of the machine shed Gayle had had earlier. "Truck broke down?"

"Just changing the oil."

"You know they got those drive-through joints now, do the whole shebang for twenty bucks and save you the mess and aggravation."

Lowell ignored this, as he'd learned to ignore ninety percent of what came out of Jack's mouth these days. Or pretended to.

"You ain't twenty-five any more," Jack resumed, "and ain't got the sense to be glad about it. Christ. Who'd be a young man in this day and age? Nary a tree worth falling, rivers all fished out, farms gone bust, cars made outa plastic and computer chips, no trespassing signs everywhere you turn, not a single war worth fighting. Way I see it, reliving our old fogey memories makes for a better life than what these poor guys coming up now are stuck with. I wouldn't be young again if you paid me time and a half!"

"You gonna drink this, now that I made it?"

Jack came over to the dinette, turned a chair around and sat on it backwards as was his habit. His legs were long enough he could do this even though he'd surely lost some stretch over the years. "Come along to the center with me, Lowell," he urged, going for the hard sell. "You've gotta get over this idea it's stepping one foot into the grave. We're a livelier bunch over there than you'd find any Saturday night at the New Peking!"

Lowell didn't try to explain that it wasn't the idea of stepping a foot into a grave that bothered him. He was ready to dive in headfirst! His aversion was to the prospect of turning into a Jack Horton, another quaint old joker in pastel "sportswear" jawing with all the other quaint old jokers about the good ol' days, maybe sucking down an Ensure over a game of pinochle and speculating on their next bowel movement. Didn't Jack remember how they used to make fun of guys like that? It wasn't so long ago. Seemed like yesterday, in fact.

"You ain't got much to say today," Jack said after a while. "It's like talking to a wall. You gonna spruce yourself up and come with me or not? It's a potluck. You look like you could use some home-cookin'."

"I got things to do," Lowell said. "I'm too busy for socializing."

Jack's snort riffled the surface of the coffee he'd lifted toward his mouth. He took a sip, thought for a long minute, then repeated his refrain, "You know the problem with you, Lowell? You're self-centered, self-indulgent and just plain selfish."

"You know where the door is," Lowell said mildly, although the truth was Jack's words stung him like baldfaced hornets.

"Whooaah, no. You can't get ridda me *that* easy. I've stood you for seventy-three years; I'm not gonna get squeamish now. But think about it: Here you are, a smart guy with plenty of miles left on ya and maybe even some wisdom to impart on the sorry state of world affairs. You play a mean game of poker and can hold your own at darts and bowling. You've got stories to tell and an ear to listen.

But will you share yourself with us poor needy souls who're desperate as hell for some new blood? Not Lowell Johnson. Lowell Johnson would sooner shrivel up and die than set foot in a place where there might be—heaven forbid!—persons of mature years enjoying each other's company."

Lowell took a sip of his coffee to hide the fact that his throat was too swollen to produce a rejoinder. Jack had left one off: self-pitying.

"Where's your sense of wonder, man!" Jack cried, slapping the dinette with the callused palm of one big hand. "Don't you know that wonders never cease, no matter how old we get! There're still things to do, people to meet, adventures to have. Sure you've had bad things happen. We all have. But there's still something to be said for life anyhow, and making the most of it. Otherwise it's plain wasteful and you oughta be ashamed."

Lowell didn't volunteer that he didn't intend to waste much more of it. He drank more coffee, pretending it was the steam that was making his eyes blink. "You're entitled to your opinions," he said eventually. "But like I said, I don't have time for socializing."

Jack narrowed his eyes as he swallowed another gulp of coffee, then smacked his lips and said, "You know the problem with you, Lowell? You've got too the hell *much* time."

✳   ✳   ✳   ✳

That night Lowell put out a grudging spoonful of Friskies Mixed Grill on a saucer on the porch. He put a kitchen chair next to the window and waited till past midnight with his .22 across his lap but the cat never showed.

Next morning the saucer was clean. Lowell felt like the victim of a con man, a real smooth operator. He had to tell himself it wasn't sensible to feel so humiliated and outsmarted by a damn cat.

In the middle of his granola his nerves were raked by one of his least favorite sounds: the ring of the telephone. It was Gayle saying a guy from the Friendly Animals place was going to drop by with the trap and tell him what to do with it. Lowell used it as an excuse to postpone confronting the oil filter for another morning.

The guy came just before noon. Lowell didn't know what to think of him. He had eyes like a doe deer and used the word "kitty" instead of "cat" without a hint of embarrassment. After explaining the proper procedure for dealing with the trapped "kitty" so it wouldn't suffer any more stress than was, unfortunately, unavoidable, he told Lowell he was on call any hour of the day or night if something went wrong.

Lowell was relieved when he left. It was hard to face this walking St. Francis when his intention was to trap the cat just long enough to shoot it.

He decided to set up the trap in the machine shed, since he had the idea that's where the tom was hiding out. He carried the tinny contraption out there, hardly tormented at all by the sight of the gaping Chevy. In fact, he felt so invigorated by being this much closer to ridding himself of the stray that he decided he'd finish the oil change right now. Then something made him glance out across the yard, and his heart bumped painfully against his breastbone.

The cat.

If he could've hidden the trap behind his back, he would have—like a schoolboy with a forbidden cigarette. It was ridiculous, the degree of dismay he felt at being caught redhanded.

The cat saw him too. No question. It rolled its big yellowy eyes his way but kept on moving, intent on what it carried in its mouth as it trotted across the rank grass toward the lilac bushes. And what was it, anyhow? Too big for a mouse. Vole? Starling? Lowell peered, then jerked back his head with a grimace. Frog, that's what. Frog or toad (he'd never been clear on the distinction; that was Virgie's department). The things dangling from the cat's jaws like a rubber fu man chu were a pair of plump frog's legs, probably the biggest Lowell had ever seen. He found himself rolling his tongue in reflexive disgust as if *he* were the one with a mouth full of amphibian. For a split second he almost felt sorry for the stray, having to stoop so low as to live off of raw frog. On the other hand, maybe it was good eatin'?

He put the trap down in the empty bay of the shed that used to house his tractor. He didn't set it. Figured he'd wait till nightfall for that. The saint from the Friends had asked him to do it right around dawn, so the kitty wouldn't have to wait long in the trap before he could drive over and transport it to the vet. This wasn't part of Lowell's plan, though. He wanted the thing caught as soon as possible and an end put to it so he could get on with putting an end to *himself*. It was that simple.

Vengeance was nigh. He felt so good about it he changed into an older pair of pants and tackled the aborted oil change job. Rolling under the engine he felt almost spry, and the filter surrendered to the first tug of the strap wrench. Fifteen minutes and the job was done and he was a renewed man. He almost could've done with one of Jack's touted home-cooked senior center meals afterwards, but settled for another bowl of granola.

*   *   *   *

Lowell set the trap at bedtime, right after dinner—his third bowl of granola of the day. Like the Friend of the Animals had instructed, he put a scoop of Mixed Grill on a lid he'd found in a drawer—a yellow plastic Hershey's syrup lid that must have dated from back when Virgie was alive, since he hadn't had anything like that in the house since then. He placed it where it needed to go in relation to the pressure plate, folded up the trapdoor and armed the latch just so. Then he went back into the house, set the alarm clock on the nightstand for midnight, and climbed into bed.

At first he thought the phone was ringing to tell him of some catastrophe, then he realized it was time and slapped the clock into silence. For a moment or two he thought *Damn. Let it wait till morning.* It was the first good night's sleep he'd had in ages. Of course, now there was no guarantee he'd recover that blissful oblivion. Besides, he wanted to dispatch the cat under cover of darkness.

He dressed, putting on his shoes and a wool pullover that was moth-eaten despite its reek of mothballs. Out in the kitchen, his .22 was waiting on the dinette. He picked it up, checked automatically to see that it was loaded, put the safety on, flipped the porch light switch and let himself out into the balmy night. In the machine shed he flipped another switch, flooding it with the indifferent illumination of the few remaining grime-smeared bulbs. He looked toward the empty bay and exultation jumped inside him. It worked! The trapdoor was down!

He almost ran a couple of strides, then stopped short, struck by a sudden doubt. *Was this the right thing to do?* Then he strode forward again, furious with himself. Was that the sort of wishy-washy thought he was going to have tomorrow night, when the target was himself? No, sir!

There was a thunk from the cage. Good! No mistake, then. It hadn't just tripped itself by accident. The cat was—

The cat wasn't.

Whatever that thing was, flinging itself against the mesh sides of the trap, it wasn't feline.

Lowell's hands automatically released the safety and took a more businesslike grip on the rifle. *What the hell?!*

It was a frog ... toad ... whatever; a huge squat goggle-eyed frog, twice as big as any he'd ever seen before. Christ! The damn cat'd had one just like that for lunch! What the hell was going on around here? Was there a whole flock of mutant amphibians taking the place over?

He reset the safety and leaned the Winchester against one of the bay's corner-posts, then knelt stiffly and gave his inadvertent captive a closer look. The frog hurled itself against the mesh again. Strange, that these creatures could lift their ungainly bodies to such heights, yet always came to earth in an unseemly splat. Where was the sense in this peculiar form of locomotion, this mix of amazing grace and remarkable clumsiness? "Now just you hold on," he said to it. "I'm gonna let you out of there. I got nothin' against *you*, even though I see you ate my bait, dammit." The Hershey's syrup lid was empty. "Serve you right if that tom-cat wants a second helping of frog legs tonight."

He opened the trap door but the frog continued to pitch itself against the back wall, so Lowell reached in and caught hold of it.

The instant that slick muscular body was in his grip, struggling in the highly melodramatic manner of frogs as if it were Faye Wray in the clutches of King Kong, he remembered a day he'd thought forever obscured beneath the scar tissue in his mind.

Sixth grade. May Day picnic.

Virginia Ann Riddle was new that year, her parents having moved up from Salem, Oregon right around December so her dad could take a job with the Coast Guard. From the moment Mrs. Coggins introduced Virginia to that room full of twelve year olds, Lowell had had his eye on her. He didn't know why. She had no shape to speak of, and female shapes had lately become an important consideration for him, or at least for Jack, whose tastes and trends Lowell codified as law. She wasn't pretty either, in any normal sense of the word, with her thick glasses and crooked mouth. Still, from the very start, whenever she happened to cross his line of sight his eyes would stick and his heart would flipflop like a hooked rainbow trout. Was it her name—Riddle—that captured his imagination? Or was it how she came in halfway through the school year and not only seemed perfectly at ease, but did nothing to wedge herself into any existing social order? She was a creature apart, like a visiting elf. It wasn't because she was shy, which was Lowell's own secret spur toward aloofness; her self-confidence and poise were eerie. It was almost as if she found people one of the less interesting of Nature's creations. Nature was her passion. He remembered the day in class that she'd declared her intention of becoming a botanist. Even those who tittered were impressed. How many twelve year olds knew what they wanted to "be" with such certainty? How many twelve year olds even knew what a botanist *was*?

By May Day, the picnic, Lowell had understood he felt something strange and powerful for the scrawny elf-girl who already needed prescription lenses for her oversized but under-endowed brown eyes. His self-prescribed regimen for curing this malady was to treat her to as much silent hostility as he could muster whenever they were thrown together, which—to his mixed relief and regret—was rarely. If she noticed, she gave no sign. He was of less interest to her than a dandelion puff, or the earwigs she might find under a stack of newspaper on the back porch.

Every year Mrs. Coggins organized a field trip picnic to her family's farm in Joyce. If it rained, they ate bag lunches sitting on hay bales in a huge gambrel barn, and relished the store-bought cake and Coca-Colas she provided. If it was sunny—as it was the year Lowell was in sixth grade—they roasted frankfurters over a stone-ringed firepit by the pond. Lowell had been having a fine old time until two things happened at once: Jack organized a little jaunt into the woods and Lowell realized he needed to relieve himself. The jaunt had been the crux of Jack's master plan. He'd started sparking with Cheryl Kendall that spring, inspiring a new craze among the more adventuresome kids in class. He and some of the other boys who had "girls" thought they might be able to steal a kiss or two in the underbrush while Mrs. Coggins was pointing out this or that childhood landmark. Lowell, being "girl"less, was supposed to be one of the ones who kept the teacher distracted. Instead, *he* was the one distracted—by the searing urgency in his bladder. He dropped farther and farther behind Mrs. Coggins and the teacher's pet types, eyeing the undergrowth with plans of his own. The problem was, by now he had no idea who was where, and was appalled at the prospect of blundering into a couple of his classmates practicing their lip-locks, or even worse, having them blunder into *him* at an inopportune moment. But equally horrifying was the idea of trying to make it all the way back up to the outhouse by the barn. What if he *didn't?*

There suddenly came the moment, though, when he wouldn't have given a damn if he'd sprinkled on the toes of Jack and Cheryl's shoes. All he cared about was getting layers of cloth out of the path of the inevitable. Relief was glorious but alas short lived before he began to worry someone might come along before he'd quite finished. No one did. And it was as he was buttoning his trousers that he saw the frog. It was sitting on a needle-tufted twig of a young fir tree he'd taken cover behind, a tiny tree frog of such vibrant unimaginable green it awoke the treasure-hunter in Lowell. Openmouthed, he reached for it like a pirate reaching into a trove of jewels. It leaped away but he caught it, and when it was safely within the confines of his cupped hands he thought, in a buzzing dreamlike way, *Virginia Riddle*. Only Virginia Riddle would know how to see this wonder he'd found.

She hadn't been on the walk Jack organized. Last Lowell had seen her, she'd been poking around the edges of the pond near where they'd had the picnic. He hurried back out of the woods into the pasture, the frog bumping against the hollows of his palms, and saw her squatting alongside the muddy bank, running her fingers through a clump of wiry shore grass in the way most girls reserved for their own hairdos. To Lowell's intense relief there was no one else around.

She didn't look up until his shadow fell across her; then she did, with preternatural calm, and said, in her always unexpectedly deep voice, "Hullo, Lowell."

"I—I've—" he began desperately, and could say no more. She'd said his name! He hadn't even been certain she knew it!

"Did you find something?" she asked, rising to her feet, bringing those soul-stabbing eyes even closer to his.

Lowell felt as though he might faint. He extended his joined hands toward her and opened them a crack. She leaned toward them and peeked. For a long moment she said and did nothing, then she tilted her face up to him and bestowed a smile that made it feel as if his feet had lifted off the soggy ground. "Were you going to drop him down my blouse, Lowell?" she asked.

Lowell reared his head back. "No! No, I never—!"

Her grin stopped him, or maybe it was the fact that she'd touched the back of his hand with the tip of one slender mud-daubed finger. "Good. I've heard boys enjoy doing things like that, but I'm quite certain frogs have better things to do, aren't you? May I hold him?"

Dizzily Lowell transferred the frog into her hands. It sat on the palm of her left while she made an amphitheater over it with her right, and although the way to escape was now clear, it didn't move except for the rapid flutter of its throat. "Prettier than an emerald," she murmured, and it struck Lowell as only to be expected that she'd stolen his own thought of a moment ago. "But I suppose we're lucky the rest of the world doesn't see it that way, or there wouldn't be any left for ordinary folks like us to pick up and look at."

And Lowell heard himself say, "*You're* not ordinary, Virginia."

She laughed at him, but in a way that made him feel good, not bad. "And you're most definitely not either," she said. "Or you would've dropped the poor thing down my blouse for sure!"

Lowell had felt then as if a warm riptide had rolled in and drawn him under, and there was no fighting it even if he'd wanted to. Which he didn't. He said, "Say, Virginia, I wonder ... would you ... I mean, do you want to maybe think about …" He dwindled off there, picturing with painful clarity the teasing he was letting himself in for, even—maybe especially—from Jack; teasing he wasn't positive his thin skin could endure. Then he looked down into Virginia Ann Riddle's eyes and said it anyhow: "Walking out sometime? That is … I mean … with *me*?"

Her expression didn't change. She continued to gaze at him, smiling, for what seemed like forever twice over. Then she turned to regard the tree frog in her cupped hands, and raising it directly in front of her face whispered, "What do *you* think?" After which she cocked her head, lifted it nearer her ear, and nodded intently, as if to imply it was answering. "Me too," she said.

It hadn't seemed unlikely at all to Lowell that Virginia and the frog were communicating, so he'd exclaimed, with a tinge of panic, "What—?"

And, curling her fingers to provide a protective railing for her tiny adviser, Virginia had taken her other rather grubby hand and slipped it into Lowell's disbelieving grasp. All she said, however, was, "Let's go find him the perfect tree."

Lowell hadn't looked at another girl—or woman—since that day, and he was fairly sure Virgie had been equally content with him. For them, it hadn't been a matter of hit and miss to get it right. For them, it had been a matter of listening to a frog.

Lowell carried the one in his hand now out into the moonlit yard and released it with a stern admonition to steer clear of cats and other miscreants. Then he went back for his .22, turned out the shed lights, and headed for the house. On the way, he heard himself chuckling, and couldn't have been more startled if the laugh had drifted to him, disembodied, on the night air. Strange, but thinking about that crucial long-ago day hadn't been the agony he would've expected. It was another kind of feeling, entirely, that he was experiencing. True, there was a certain sting, but there was also a sense of release. It was like a festering splinter had been pulled out of his vitals. Shaking his head, he chuckled again and said out loud, "I'll be damned. Wonder how that thing got in there? I didn't know frogs ate cat foo—"

He stopped short, one foot on the bottom step of the back porch. The cat was perched on the railing above him, licking its chops as if it had just finished off a juicy bit of beef.

By the time Lowell jerked the rifle butt to his shoulder, it had dived off the porch and vanished like a wisp of living smoke into the darkness.

"Damn," Lowell swore. It would've been a fine way to cap this bizarre topsy-turvy day.

*   *   *   *

He baited the trap the following night at about ten, spooning another stinky lump of Friskies onto the yellow lid. After an extra bowl of granola—for some reason the one at dinner hadn't quite appeased his belly—he sat in a dark kitchen with the back door cracked and the rifle across his lap. He thought he might be able to hear the trap clatter shut, and save himself from having to wake in the middle of the night.

He was right. It wasn't fifteen minutes before he heard a sound like two old-fashioned metal shopping carts being shoved together. If it wasn't the trap he didn't know what else it could be, and he'd better check it out anyhow.

Charged with a gleeful energy, he carried the .22 out to the shed and flipped on the light. As he rounded the front of his truck he saw to his dismay that the trap in the neighboring bay was indeed sprung, but it was also empty. *Must've been the wind*, he thought, blaming a familiar villain. He leaned the rifle against the post again and went on, cussing. He sure hoped the thing hadn't come clanging down when the cat came around sniffing, and scared it off. How many nights was this gonna take? He had better things to do than sit up waiting for a …

By then he was standing over the trap, and discovering it wasn't empty after all.

It was like being tackled by an invisible linebacker. Something struck him full in the chest, hard enough to expel all the air in his lungs, and he staggered back a half step before finding a hasty route to his knees. There he waited a minute, hyperventilating, cobwebs of dizziness filming his eyes, before in a sudden scramble he opened the trap door and grabbed the thing inside.

Closing his fingers around it he couldn't help closing his eyes too, and when he opened them again a trickle of hot liquid seeped over each lower lid. With a faint wheezing sob, he held the thing in front of him and stared at it as if he intended to hypnotize himself.

The tarnished silver horse galloped furiously in place as it twisted at the end of the brief loop of chain. The chain connected the replica to the two dirt-encrusted keys in Lowell's trembling fingers. The keys to his son's Mustang.

There were only two points on which Jeremy Johnson had ever defied his father—or at least taken a different tack. One was over guns. He'd join Lowell in target practice all day long, but when it came to hunting … not interested. The other was on choosing to own a Ford over a Chevy. However, even Lowell had to admit to being smitten by the black beauty Jeremy had ended up with, after slaving and saving from the time he was eleven. The dream hadn't always been a Mustang, of course. He'd gone through some passionate affairs with Ferraris and Corvettes. But then the Mustang had come along, and Jeremy was shy only a couple hundred bucks which Lowell gladly loaned him, knowing without a doubt his son would pay him back with interest, because that was the kind of stubbornly over-responsible kid Jeremy was. They couldn't have afforded the car under *any* circumstances had it been new, but it was four years old and had known some rough treatment at the hands of its frat boy owner, so they'd gotten a good deal. And then, between the two of them, tweaked and polished it into the envy of the county.

If any kid deserved such a car, though, it was Jeremy. Never once had he done a thing to make his parents worry or feel an ounce of shame. While other boys were driving drunk and getting girls in trouble, he was helping his dad patch the roof or his mom till the garden. While Gayle was reading inflammatory books and saying inflammatory things to anyone who'd listen (and chanting them at the ones who wouldn't), Jeremy was saving for his dream car, working earnestly on his grades, excelling at baseball, and expressing a genuine, uncoerced desire to follow in the footsteps of his old man.

No one could have asked for a better son.

Lowell stared at the tiny Mustang, remembering. Remembering how he'd kept his eyes fixed on that polished steed, dangling from the ignition, when he and Jeremy sat in the car outside Lehman's discussing the letter from the Draft Board. Remembered how hard it'd been for him to say, without coming right out and using the words, that he didn't want Jeremy to go. Other fathers' egos might not be equal to having a son labeled traitor or coward, but Lowell knew his feelings for his boy could never run so shallow. "Don't do it for my sake," he recalled saying, after a long conversation where nothing he was getting at in theory got out in practice. "Do what you think is right, and I'll be behind you one hundred percent." (One of the great regrets of his life was that he only seemed capable of expressing emotion via fatuous clichés, as if he'd learned to feel through a TV antenna.) Lowell's fervent hope had been that Jeremy would think Canada was right, or even prison, but he hadn't said that part out loud. Maybe that had been his mistake?

Then again, maybe it wouldn't have made any difference. Jeremy had sounded mighty firm when he said, "I'm going, Dad. I have to. Not because I think it's my duty, and not because I'm scared not to 'cause of what people would say. It's just ... why should I think *I'm* so special?"

Because you *are*! Lowell had wanted to yell. For once he'd wanted to say, Be more like your sister! Rebel for rebellion's sake, if nothing else! God knows there's reason enough to protest this damn mess in Vietnam. Everybody's doing it! Congressmen, movie stars. Why not you!

But the boy had made his decision and Lowell couldn't see a way of talking him out of it. "Besides, Dad," he'd said, with one of his serious smiles, "how much longer can it go on?"

It had gone on another eight months between that day and the day Jeremy was set down from a helicopter near a rice paddy outside a village whose name Lowell had never learned to pronounce.

It had gone on another few seconds after that, when three rounds from a sniper's rifle had exploded his lungs.

Right after they got word, Lowell had grabbed the Mustang's keys thinking—if that's what you'd call it—thinking he'd drive it until the smothering pain lifted the hell off him. Then Virgie had come out on the porch after him, her face blotched and damp. She didn't clutch or question, only said one word: "Don't." So he'd wrenched back his arm and thrown the keychain with all his might, not even watching where it went, then turned and pulled her against him. It was the first time they'd ever had to cry together.

Weeks later when he'd gathered the courage to look for the keys Lowell hadn't found them. In '85, when he finally agreed to sell the Mustang, they'd had to pull the spare set off the peg in the mud room to let the guy test drive it. It ran like a top, as well it should considering the attention Lowell had lavished on it for fourteen years. That was the problem: Virgie'd got it into her head it was morbid to keep the car. Jeremy wouldn't have wanted a shrine, she said. He would've wanted it to go to a fellow enthusiast, not sit in the garage keeping wounds open. Lowell had realized, then, that the real reason she wanted it sold was she was worried sick about him 'cause he wouldn't leave it alone. The car … his dead son … Vietnam—any of it. Lowell didn't like to make Virgie worry, so he let it go.

And now here were those keys, missing for so long. Found.

How? The frog was one thing. There was a logical explanation for that. A frog as large as that could easily trip the cage same as a cat would, and if it wasn't the Friskies that had lured it in, maybe it'd hopped that way by accident, then eaten the food because it was trapped and that was all there was.

But how could an inanimate handful of metal and memory find its way inside a sprung trap? Was it dropped in, maybe? Lowell spent a moment trying to force the keychain through the steel mesh but there was no way it would go. Too big, no matter the angle. Then he searched every inch of the cage, looking for places where the wires had been pushed wider. Nothing.

The hair on his nape and forearms prickled. It had to be that someone was doing this to him on purpose. Unless—He wiped the sweat from his upper lip. Could it be him*self*? Had he gone round the bend? Had he come across the keys and the shock put him into a daze, split him into another personality for a while, and he'd decided to play this trick on himself? He couldn't see it. For one thing, he knew he wasn't crazy. Maybe that sounded funny, coming from a man who had every intention of killing himself as soon as he'd dealt with the nuisance of a stray tomcat, but as far as he was concerned suicide was proof of his enduring common sense. If you can't stand the heat, get outa the kitchen. If life has nothing to offer, shuffle off the mortal coil and make room for those who do enjoy it. He'd have done exactly that days ago if not for the damn cat.

He started, sensing surveillance. Twisting his head he found the cat sitting on the edge of the island of light thrown by the machine shed bulbs, staring thoughtfully at him, its tail curled around its legs. It looked quite a bit sleeker than last time, its head no longer so oversized and misshapen. In fact, its appearance was almost dapper. As Lowell stared, transfixed, it stretched wide its jaws and ran a salmon-pink tongue around them, after which it stood, flicked its tail, and raced off across the yard to disappear into the high grass of the orchard.

Lowell remembered, then, to look at the chocolate syrup lid. The lump of Friskies was not only gone, the lid looked as if it had been licked to a shine.

He struggled to his feet, heart thudding, head spinning. Clutching the keychain he ran in a broken hobbling fashion toward the porch. There, he remembered the gun. Leave it! No. With his mind so full of his responsible-to-a-fault son, he couldn't bear to disgrace the memory by behaving irresponsibly himself. He went back for the Winchester and shut out the shed lights before returning to the house, forced to move slowly now because of the total absence of light. Inside the kitchen door he groped for the switch, and released a shaky sigh when everything appeared perfectly normal there. Everything made sense but the keychain clenched in his hand. Unwilling to part from it lest it vanish like his son had, he carried it with him while he locked up the gun, then returned to the kitchen, got a dishcloth out of a drawer, and began to rub the dirt out of every crevice.

For hours he polished away, thinking about his son … remembering … thanking heaven that in the short time they'd had together no bitterness had ever passed between them, no disappointment. No borderline hatred, like had cropped up between poor Jack and his son Cory. Jeremy and Cory had grown up together, although they were never particularly good friends, what with Jeremy's rather square pursuits and attitudes. Cory had come back from Vietnam alive. Lowell could remember the horrible resentment he'd felt toward Jack over that, but as things turned out … If Jeremy had come back would *he* have been as altered as Cory? Lowell shook his head. It wouldn't have mattered. He and Virgie would've welcomed their son home gladly, no matter what wounds the war had inflicted upon him. And perhaps, like Jack, they would've watched their boy get swallowed up by the worst in the world, unable to do anything about it. There was no way of knowing, now.

At long last Lowell stumbled off to his bedroom, still clutching the Mustang's keys. There, he set them on the chest of drawers next to the framed photo of Virgie in her floppy hat holding the largest zucchini her garden had ever produced. The shot was black and white; she'd never cared for color ones except of her flowers, and she was standing in front of a row of pole peas.

He lifted the picture by its well-worn frame and in a hoarse whisper told her what he'd found, where and how. Speaking to her was nothing new, but as he did it now he felt a strange sensation that this time … *this time* … she might speak back. He hardly dared to breathe. His racing heart had whipped his blood to a froth. For a long moment after he'd fallen silent he waited. Then there rose in him an urge to say something else, foolish and dangerous as it was. "Is it you, Virgie?" he asked plaintively. "Is it … is all this a message of some kind?"

Virgie smiled at him from the photograph as she always had. That was all. And yet Lowell felt deeply peaceful as he set the picture down next to the keychain. Why, he couldn't have said to save his life. He supposed it was how the religious felt when they truly believed, and still he had no sense of the presence of any god. Just Virgie, smiling, cradling that gigantic zucchini.

Later, lying in bed in the dark, he thought more about his son. Not the regrets, not the horrors, but the things that made him swell with pride and thankfulness. For nineteen years he'd had the privilege of knowing an exceptional human being. He would always wish there'd been more years, and he would always detest the warmongers who'd stolen the lives of his son and Cory and so many others. But for whatever time he had left there was no sense in denying himself the recollection of the good years for fear of reawakening the bad. The bad, after all, never truly slept. Let the good have a chance at the light now and then.

So he let himself remember, for instance, the time Jeremy had begged to help him replace a head gasket on their old truck when he was nine years old. His instinct for motors, his love for them, had been as unshakable as Lowell's. And the thing was, he'd *been* a help, and by the time he was fourteen could've done the job alone.

And now here was this Xavier kid, his grandson, supposedly telling his mom he wanted to learn to work on cars. Was it possible the family madness had found its next host in the new generation?

Lowell yawned and rolled over onto his side, finally feeling the soft nibble of drowsiness at the edges of his brain. Maybe he'd tell Gayle to bring the kid on over this coming weekend, and he'd show him what a *real* engine looked like, not a tangle of wires and microchips like these Cracker Jack toys on the road nowadays. No nephew of Jeremy's and no grandson of *his* was gonna reach manhood without knowing how to change his own oil!

He could wait a few more days to put his plan in motion. Besides, there was still that cat to deal with.

*   *   *   *

First thing next morning, Lowell got some tools out of the gardening shed and dug up the weeds around the flowering crab under which Virgie's ashes were buried. It was scandalous, how he'd let the orchard grass and dandelions encroach, threatening to choke out the tree. It was woefully undersized for its seven years in the ground. If Virgie had been tending it, it would've been a different story. Best prepare the soil a bit, he figured, so it'd be easier for Gayle to dig in his own ashes when the time came. And in the meantime, it'd be easier to water and fertilize the living memorial Virgie had wanted.

He worked at it from dawn to well after noon, then, aching in an unaccustomed but almost pleasant way and slick with honest sweat, he went into the house and washed his hands at the kitchen sink, gazing out the window at the gratifyingly visible fruits of his labor. The tree looked worlds happier already, with that apron of clean brown dirt beneath it. He'd taken up the weeds clear back to the drip-line. Maybe he'd go to the Co-op today, pick up some sacks of manure and mulch. Maybe even one of those little ready-made wooden picket fences that came in sections.

Drying his hands, he realized the ache in his stomach came from honest hunger. It had been a long time since he'd felt such a concerted demand from his belly. He got the granola down from the cupboard and was reaching into the fridge for the milk when he saw the package of bacon in the meat drawer. He considered, then rejected, the idea of frying up a slice or two. He did, however, take out the carton of orange juice as well as the milk, because all that sweating had left him with a raging thirst. He shook it up and poured himself a tall glass, marveling at the color. Nature came up with the most astounding things.

This made him think of the mystery of the keychain again, but since he wasn't any nearer to explaining it to himself he just stood there shaking his head. Jack accused him of having lost his sense of wonder. Well, he was damn sure wondering *now*, not that it was doing him an ounce of good. Or was it? Last night he'd slept as well as he had in years, and this morning he'd woken up with Virgie and Jeremy all around him, pervading the very air like the smell of new-mown alfalfa used to do in late summer when he was a kid; woken up with crazy schemes of spending the day weeding the garden and dusting his dashboard.

Lowell carried the glass of juice over to the sink so he could observe his handiwork again, and through the window he saw the cat picking its way across the painstakingly hand-dug soil, sniffing intently at the clods.

He slammed his glass down on the counter so hard he was lucky it didn't shatter, and rapped thunderously on the pane. Then he charged for the door and raged out onto the porch, down the stairs, and across the yard toward Virgie's tree.

Unimpressed by the oncoming juggernaut, the cat stayed where it was until Lowell was but two yards away, regarding him with an expression of bemusement or disdain. Then it whipped around and streaked off toward the machine shed.

Lowell staggered to a halt, braced his hands on his wobbly knees and hunched over, panting, still seeing the world through a ruddy veil. Then, fuming, he began to look for the damage. Damn cat. They couldn't pass a patch of clean friable soil without wanting to defile it in some way. Even Virgie had said as much. Virgie, who loved cats despite what they tended to do in her garden. She'd thought it was something worth putting up with, for the joys of feline companionship. Lowell was of a different opinion. No way was that cat gonna be free to mess on Virgie's grave!

He found no desecration, thank goodness. He'd apparently gotten there in time.

*   *   *   *

It was tempting to stand guard over the tree with his gun all night, but Lowell had the sense this would be doing something not quite right-in-the-head, so he resolved to try the trap one more time. He opened a new can of Friskies, since the remnants of the old had grown stale in the fridge. The Friend of the Animals had stressed that the smellier the bait, the better. This new stuff made Lowell want to gag, but maybe this could also be blamed on the fact that he'd been too agitated to eat all day. That few swallows of orange juice was all he'd been able to get down, thanks to the cat's latest transgression.

He set the alarm for midnight again, but this time was still wide awake when it went off, lying on top of the blankets fully dressed but for his shoes, which he grimly put on. Picking up the .22, ready and waiting on the table, he let himself out into the night and with firm strides, as inexorable as Death itself, he stalked out to the machine shed.

The trap had been sprung. By now he was used to finding that. What made his heart pound with such queer emphasis was thinking what he might find inside. Blinking, he hesitated, tuning his eyes. There was no movement, no sound from the rectangle of mesh. He moved nearer, swallowing with a dry throat. He wasn't frightened exactly. Or maybe he *was*. But the heart of his fear was that, this time, he'd find nothing at all.

Which appeared to be the case. This time the wind really must have done it. He took another step ... and saw.

Lowell dropped the rifle and was aware of a distant relief that the safety was on. Then he lowered himself carefully to his knees and bent forward till his forehead almost touched the cage's metal roof. He didn't reach for it, though. For now, he could only look and try to absorb what he was seeing.

Inside the sprung trap was the yellow plastic Hershey's syrup lid. The spoonful of cat food was gone. In its place lay a dirt-encrusted locket on a broken chain. Virgie's locket. The one Gayle had given her on a Mother's Day when Gayle was no more than ten. She'd gotten it through a schoolmate's mother, who sold Avon, and hadn't paid more than five dollars for it, but Virgie couldn't have appreciated it any more if it had been real gold. Inside, Lowell knew he would find two pared down school photographs, one of Gayle, one of Jeremy, the latter having been inserted over the objections of Gayle, who'd figured the family dog, Hoot, was more photogenic than her little brother.

Lowell felt very light, as if he'd been scooped out and was waiting for something all-new to fill him. For once his seventy-three year old joints didn't protest the contortions he was demanding of them. He knelt over that cage and its trapped locket like an entranced child over his first wooly-bear caterpillar.

He remembered the day Virgie'd lost it, coming in from the yard in an unusual state of fluster, furious with herself for having forgotten and worn it outside to work in. Earlier she'd dressed up to go to brunch with some old friends from college, fellow botany majors, and come back so eager to get her fingers back into their element all she'd done was change her shoes. She'd only planned to deadhead the rhodies, but then she'd seen some thistles starting up out in the lawn …

Together they'd spent the rest of that afternoon looking for the locket, mostly in the spot Virgie remembered slapping at the back of her neck, thinking something was crawling on her, and now wondered if it might've been the chain, newly broken, slithering off. For hours they were on their hands and knees, patting and pawing through the grass.

Hours on their knees, in exactly the same place Lowell had spent hours on his knees today, clearing the weed-choked sod from around Virgie's memorial tree.

They'd never found the locket. Obviously. But now somebody—some*thing*—had, and given it back to him. Another piece of Virgie to keep. A tangible memory, like the keychain, like the frog.

Later, Lowell had no clear recollection of taking the locket out of the cage and going into the house with it. Or of cleaning it off as meticulously as he had the keys. Or of verifying the tiny photographs within, still recognizable, still packing a punch to his heart. Or of placing the locket on the chest of drawers next to the keys, and kissing the framed picture of Virgie. Or of climbing back into bed.

However, he remembered tumbling into a dream where he and Virgie were digging in the garden and along the row behind them came a gaunt gray cat, sniffing at beetles and pouncing on butterflies, and Virgie smiled and said, "Let him be, Lowell. He's only trying to find a present for us."

"What sort of present?" the dream-Lowell had demanded, picturing decapitated mice deposited on thresholds.

And the dream-Virgie had grinned her crooked grin and said, "The kind to go with our past, of course."

When he woke to a room shimmering with sunlight, the fog had cleared and there was a whole thought, clearly formulated, waiting to be scrutinized.

It was this: Jack was right. Wonders never ceased. And it was a damn sorry sight when a man decided to stop appreciating any that came his way.

Immediately afterwards, he leapt from bed reaching for his clothes. He'd forgotten the gun. It was lying out there, loaded, in the shed.

The day outside was the kind that made you look twice at what was ordinarily taken for granted. The arcing blue sky, the snow-laced Olympics beyond the subdivision to the south, standing out with the newly washed clarity they rarely showed once the sun turned its full glare upon them. Starlings had taken over a mountain ash on his property line and wanted the whole world to hear about it. A covey of quails scurried willy-nilly across his driveway before exploding into belated flight, alarmed by his march toward the shed. He could smell mown grass, pine needles, and the earth he'd dug up around the flowering crab tree. Like his joints, his eyes, ears, and nose were working better than they had in ages.

Then when he reached the machine shed he saw that the trap had been sprung again. He'd neither baited it nor set it, and yet there it was. And lying neatly inside it was the cat, as inscrutable as the Sphinx, watching his approach out of huge yellow-green eyes as if it had been waiting there for him for years.

The Winchester, loaded, was lying right there. Lowell looked at it, then back at the cat, who blinked once but only once and continued its yellow stare.

Lowell walked over to the cage and got carefully to his knees. The cat sat up, but far from showing any alarm at his nearness, indulged in an extravagant yawn.

Lowell opened the trap. The cat remained sitting inside, regarding him as calmly as ever.

For about half a minute, that's where things stood.

Then the cat rose and stepped to the front of the cage. Lowell felt like a door-man as it paused there, gazing left and right like a penthouse swell. Then it stepped forward and placed first one front paw, then the other, on Lowell's bent knee. And tilting back its head, it gazed straight into Lowell's eyes and said—

"Mraow?"

Lowell gazed back. A moment passed. Two. Then he said, in a voice as scuffed as his old shoes, "Well there, Finder. How do you feel about scrambled eggs and bacon?"

Erika Hamerquist has been writing stories and novels since she was seven years old. Won't someone please make her stop?! She lives with three horses, six cats, and four foster dogs in Sequim, Washington.

© Raven 2007

GREYLING

Raven O'Keefe

ANATOMY LESSON AT YOUNG'S DAIRY

by Morgan Van Dyke

Last week Julie, my niece, along with her husband, Brad, and their two young sons, Zach and Eli, went to Young's Dairy. Young's is a home grown dairy that caters to locals just on the outskirts of Yellow Springs, Ohio, about a half hour ride east of Dayton and close to the fabulous John Bryant State Park. Members of our clan have gone there for years to play on retired tractors, feed the farm animals and eat home made ice cream. The farm is so popular there is always at least a small crowd of people not only from Ohio, but folks from across the country and even the oceans. Little did Julie know that a trouble-free spring day and a fun visit to the dairy would turn into an anatomy lesson for everyone in close proximity to the barn.

Zach, age four, pulled his mother into the Visitors' Barn. Brad followed behind carrying baby Eli. They were surrounded by the fecund smells of fresh hay, cows and goats. Zach continued tugging his mother's arm until they reached the pens where goats beg for nibbles of food and head scratches. Dancing with excitement, he pointed to the animal in the nearest stall. "Momma, look at that goat's big wiener!"

Julie's face heated, and she tried to ignore the titters of the people around her. She squatted next to Zach and said as quietly and calmly as she could, "No, honey, that's a mommy goat. She feeds her baby from her boobies. That's where her milk comes from."

She watched her son's face, and when she thought he'd absorbed what she'd said, she gave him a quick hug and brushed the hair from his eyes. "Come on," she said standing and taking his small hand. "Let's look in the next pen."

She and Zach watched the animals in the next cage, the little boy studying them intently.

"Look, Momma," Zach piped up. He pointed. "Look. That goat has two wieners."

Chagrined, Julie took another stab at correcting him. "Ummm … no baby. Those are boobies." She was acutely aware of the muffled chuckling of those strangers close at hand.

Zach glared up at her, hands on his hips. "No, Momma. YOU have BOO-BIES," he broadcast rather loudly and with assurance.

Guffaws erupted around her. Julie thought she could hear her husband's laughter in the mix. Sure enough, when she glanced over her shoulder, she saw him, a grin on his face and his eyes tearing. She noticed that Brad stood at a safe distance. After the laughter died down and the strangers moved on, he sidled up and whispered, "Good going. Distract him and maybe he'll never bring it up again."

"Smart ass," she hissed back. *A little help here would be appreciated,* she thought. Before Brad had a chance to react, a determined Zach was already pulling her toward the next stall … and then to the next, pointing out "wieners" along the way.

They finally made it through the barn to the pens on the outside. There in broad daylight was a magnificent bull.

In awe, Zach bent over and almost turned upside down to look. Finally he righted himself and shook his little head like something had just clicked. He smiled to his mother and loudly proclaimed, "Momma, LOOK at that cow's BOOBIES!"

Julie took a deep breath and rolled her eyes heavenward, "Yes, baby. Look at those boobies!"

Behind her she could hear applause and unrestrained laughter.

Morgan Van Dyke lives in Gardiner, Washington, with her spouse, Elizabeth, and their border collie companion, Flash. She started writing psychological thrillers to help her deprogram from her former career as a psychotherapist. Physician heal thyself—and a dog helps too.

© Raven 2007

MOSS & MINNIE

Raven O'Keefe

DIVINE FELINE

by Susan M. Skaggs

It was a dark and stormy night when the cat spoke. I'd been home from work less than fifteen minutes and was dozing in my ratty old recliner, when the doorbell rang.

I stumbled to the door and plopped a handful of candy into the trick-or-treat bag of a furry crocodile who waited on my porch looking cold and damp. I got the feeling it was missing the tropics as it turned and waddled off into the night.

The unruly gray hair at my temples, the first to discolor the brown and give evidence of forty-five hard years, blew across my eyes making me feel witchy. I slammed the door shut. Under my breath, I cursed my boss for insisting I distribute the Halloween candy left over from the office party. Children swamped my neighborhood every October 31st, making my house a perfect spot for getting rid of cheap sugar highs. Besides, he was worried about me. "Ravinia," he'd said, "It will do you good."

I cursed a little louder. I needed sleep. I was depressed. I was broke. I had an empty nest. Cute kids in costumes only made me feel worse. I certainly didn't need Halloween.

I also didn't need the cat. I hated cats. I'd refused to have one in the house ever since I'd heard they sucked the breath from babies. I didn't mind dogs. They could be placated with biscuits, something I habitually carried in my coat pocket for the ones in my neighborhood.

I glared at the Siamese sitting haughtily in the middle of my living room. It glared back-blue eyes in a chocolate face. It had been a gift from my daughter, Crystal, who'd found it as a stray and couldn't keep it in her dorm room. She said it would do me good. She was worried about me.

Everyone was worried about me. *I* was worried about me. Ever since Crystal and her twin brother, Chris, had left for college, I'd been in a funk. Everything was backwards. When I needed to sleep, I couldn't. When I needed to be awake, I was dropping off like a narcoleptic. My appetite had grown just as fickle. Almost as fickle as the damn cat's.

Sighing, I slumped back into the recliner. On top of everything else, I felt guilty. I hadn't meant to make Crystal worry. It was supposed to work the other way around: parent as worrier, kid as worrisome. Everything was backwards.

I was asleep again in seconds, dreaming of catless houses and designer clothes I couldn't afford.

We wish to go out.

I surfaced from the dream, confused and disoriented as the high-pitched, nasal voice penetrated my consciousness. *We wish to go out. You will open the door.*

I glanced around. No one else was in the room. I blinked and gave my head a brisk shake. Over-tired from working two jobs to put two kids through college at the same time, I'd simply had a very vivid dream.

We wish to go out.

My heart jumped into my throat and lodged there. Wait a minute. I was awake this time. I was absolutely sure. Almost.

The cat was sitting on the floor in front of me. I stared at it, and it looked up from daintily washing the toes on one outstretched foot, its expression rife with scorn. *Are you listening, woman? Open the door.*

I leapt up from the recliner, spilling candy onto the threadbare carpet. Gathering Tootsie Rolls and Hershey bars, I tried to regain my wits. The cat was talking. It couldn't be. I was still asleep. This was still a dream. I opened the door in a daze. I pinched myself hard, which I understood was the thing to do in times like these. It hurt. I wasn't dreaming. Oh, God.

Good help is so difficult to find, the cat muttered as it strode through the doorway, tail erect. It glanced back over its shoulder and tilted its head toward me as it reached the bottom step. *We will be back in fifteen minutes. You will have the door open when we return.*

It bounded from the step and disappeared into the wind and rain.

Closing the door, I leaned against it. I brushed my slacks, picking out tiny cat hairs as if the action would remove the hallucination from my life. My depression must have blossomed into full-blown psychosis. I had to do something. But what?

The doorbell rang, almost causing me to toss the candy again. I cautiously eased the door open. A child carrying his head in his hands stood on my front stoop. Someone had stuffed the jacket and positioned the arms and a pair of gloves at the front of the coat. The boy now peeked from between those fake arms.

"Nice costume," I mumbled, absentmindedly pouring candy into the canvas grocery bag he held with fingers sneaking from beneath the bottom edge of his jacket.

The cat was nowhere to be seen. Minutes passed as I stood there gazing wild-eyed into darkness. I was going crazy. No, I'd already gone. The hearing voices part proved it.

At last I saw the cat striding regally into the circle of light from my porch bulb.

"You're back," I said inanely.

It flicked its dark ears and regarded me in an aloof manner, blue eyes slightly crossed. *Of course we are back. We said we would return.*

I couldn't tell how it was speaking to me. I just knew I was hearing it whether I wished to or not. It walked into the living room, jumped up, and perched on the scarred end-table next to the recliner. *We wish to speak to you about your mission.*

"My mission?" I hadn't a clue what it was talking about, but at this point I didn't have many clues left about anything in my dizzy brain.

It is All Hallows' Eve.

"All Hallows' Eve?"

You will stop repeating our words.

"Your words?"

I could almost see the cat gritting its teeth. *Stop it! Nnyow!* Its command was punctuated by a loud and distinctive Siamese yowl. That, at least, definitely reached me through my ears.

I slammed my jaw shut. God knew what a six pound furry hallucination could do to a full grown woman. I didn't want to find out.

The world of the dead and the world of the living are close together.

"Togeth …" I reined the word in just in time. The cat slanted me a hard look.

We must journey to Hades. You will assist us.

"To hell in a cat basket," I muttered as I crossed to the telephone just inside the dining room. The cat could talk all it wanted; I wouldn't listen. And I certainly wouldn't accompany it to hell. The thought crossed my mind I might already be there. I shook my head. It was important to remember that there was such a thing as reality.

"You're a cat. You can't talk," I said firmly. "So stop it. Right nnyow!"

I rummaged through the orange crate that served as phone stand. "You're a cat. You can't talk," I said as I thumbed through the yellow pages to T for therapist. "I'm human. I talk. but not to talking cats. So there."

The cat growled. *Cease this scrambling at once.* It sauntered over and stood at my feet, scowling up at me. *Compose yourself, woman.*

"Psychiatrists are expensive," I mumbled, setting down the phone book in sudden horror. I could ignore the voice. I knew I could. "With two kids in college, I can't afford a bus pass, let alone a shrink." But then I shook my head and picked up the directory again. "No, I can't let this go. I have to think of the children." I started pawing toward the T's as hysteria loomed.

You need no therapist. You need to come with us. There is a door to the underworld we cannot open.

"I'm not talking to you, cat," I snapped, slapping the orange crate with the phone book for emphasis. "I won't. I won't. You're not real. You can't talk. This is all an illusion. It's—"

The cat yowled again and lashed out with half-inch claws, catching my skin between pant leg and loafer. I gasped, then fell silent, stunned to obedience.

Enough. You are being impertinent. You will not call us cat. Furthermore, you will use soothing tones upon addressing us, and if we seek transportation or massage, you will instantly provide it.

The cat jumped to the top of the sideboard and paced back and forth, knocking off pencils and packs of post-it notes I'd left scattered there. It lifted a dark paw within striking distance of the dining room curtains at the window.

I leapt to stop it. Those were my grandmother's curtains. I grabbed the cat before it could slice a gash down the middle of the fabric.

It nestled against my chest. *Yes. Exactly,* it purred. *And in addition you will not call us cat. You may call us Majesty, if you wish. Your Highness is also appropriate. Divine Feline has a nice ring to it. Precious will do, if you are of a maudlin disposition.*

My daughter called it Princess, I remembered. She'd draped the cat over my shoulder when she'd arrived for her last visit, saying, "Princess needs a good home, Mom. She'll cheer you up. You'll be good for each other."

Well the cat cheered me up about as much as a dentist's drill. I put it down warily.

Now, the cat said, *we will go.* It padded to the front door. *Come.*

I grabbed my jacket. Maybe the rain would clear my head, and at least if the cat were outside, it couldn't destroy my house. Not that there was much left to destroy. The kids had already done a tolerably good job of ruining anything of value.

We headed into the driving rain, the cat twitching its tail with impatience.

A gray Persian, its long fur wet and matted, joined us, gliding silently beside the Siamese. My head felt no clearer. I seemed unable to do anything but follow the cat. Cats, now.

You will open the door, the Siamese said. It stood on its back legs stretching its lithe frame against a jumble of boards inclined against a blackberry bramble.

"That isn't a door," I said. "It's a ..."

My words died as I looked again. In the wind and darkness the wood did have a rectangular outline, and there was a circle midway down the right side that might almost be a latch. I stepped closer, realizing that what I had assumed to be a pile of lumber was some sort of shed within the jumble of brambles.

Majesty, the Persian said. *Are you sure this is the right human for the job? She seems a trifle ...* It hesitated as though searching for the correct word. *Ah ... bird-brained.*

I resented that. I ran my fingers along the dark door. "It has a deadbolt. No wonder you couldn't open it."

I gripped the lever and strained against the rusted lock until it snicked, wondering why the lock had been installed backwards. But what did I know about hallucinating? I was new to insanity.

The door suddenly gave, and I catapulted forward catching myself as *Her Majesty* padded by me, the Persian on her tail. Several other feline forms streaked by and disappeared into the darkness. What was this? Cat commandos?

"You could at least have said thank you," I groused under my breath.

Two glowing eyes stared up at me from the tunnel. *Come,* Her Majesty ordered. *There may be other doors.*

"Now wait a minute. I didn't sign on for—"

She yowled. I obeyed. I poked a tentative toe forward and felt a stairstep. Damn, the hallucination had a basement.

More cats swarmed around me and down the stairs, disappearing into the dark. Blindly I followed, wondering if it was better to give in to insanity or fight it. What would Freud say? When I reached the bottom (I hoped), I stepped forward with my hands raised before me and immediately collided with something solid but repulsively slimy. Not a nice combination. I lurched back, trying to shake the goo from my fingers.

It is another door, the cat said. *Open it.*

Oh right. Let *me* mess up *my* hands while she kept her paws clean.

Open it. I could almost hear her unsheathing her claws.

I groped squeamishly through the gunk until I found what I thought was a handle. I turned it, my fingers slipping, and pushed. The door opened into a passage flooded with light. Blinking, I stared down a narrow hallway lined with river rock. Cats brushed by me.

"Where are we going?" I whispered.

To rescue the steward, a tom with battle-scarred ears volunteered.

"The steward?"

Her Majesty turned to glower at me.

He was taken last All Hallows' Eve, the Persian said.

By the Lord of the Underworld. This from a tiny ginger-colored female.

On the night when the doors of the dead will open, said a tabby-colored cat with a black spot on his nose.

"The steward is?" I asked.

Enough, Her Majesty growled. *We have no time to waste.*

She trotted off, the others following. I hurried to keep up, wondering why I was giving in to dementia so easily. I had been a stolid child and a sensible teen. Now I was turning into a loopy middle-aged woman, and I hadn't even hit menopause yet! Where was the sense in that?

You may know the steward as the King of Cats, the ginger informed me.

He isn't king, the battered tom said. *He is our chief steward, as his father was, and his father before him.*

I didn't understand much of what they said. That is, the words were crystal-clear. It was the concepts that escaped me. Doors to the underworld. Stewards. It was all nonsense. But then, this was the first time I'd ever been psychotic. Maybe I'd get the hang of it as I went along.

The corridor curved and I found myself staring into a large room. It was cold and damp. The overwhelming odor of unchanged kitty litter insulted my sinuses. My shoes made a sucking sound on the sticky floor as I walked out into the chamber. Along one white-washed wall, row upon row of cat carriers stretched floor to ceiling. Most were empty, their doors open. A few held furred shapes moving listlessly in the shadowy confines.

"Where are we?" I whispered.

In cat hell, the tiny ginger said.

"Why are all these cages empty?"

The Persian stared. *Because there are so few bad cats.* His frown added "bird-brain."

A tall human with a bulldog jaw turned from one of the crates. I saw the word "Vet" embroidered on his jacket. I stepped back into the tunnel, not sure whether I should allow the man to see me, particularly after I noticed the tail protruding from the hem of his lab coat. At his feet, a herd of Chihuahuas, pugs and rat terriers snapped. Their high-pitched yapping grated on my nerves.

The vet glided through the canine cacophony to one of the cages directly across the room from my hiding place and flourished a thermometer. There was a shriek, and the dog-man recorded something on his clipboard.

Suddenly there was an eruption of screams and giggles from the far side of the cavernous room. A small boy and girl sucking oversized lollipops tore past the vet in pursuit of a large bobcat-like cat. Its brown fur bore red daubs of drooled high fructose corn syrup.

The Cat of the Baskervilles, the Persian told me as the children shrieked by. *He made the hound look saintly.*

The children turned at his words and homed in on us. I stepped between them and the cats. "Hey, you kids. Don't run with those things in your mouths!" I said sternly. "You'll choke. Or put your eye out."

The little demons stopped in confusion, then cackled, clutched their lollies and ran off after the Cat of the Baskervilles once more.

Well done, Her Majesty hissed, and shuddered her pearl grey shoulders. *Hell is even worse than we imagined.* She and the rest of the felines were gathered round my ankles, their bodies so tight against my legs I could barely move. *Do you see the steward?* she asked.

I drew my coat tighter to ward off the chill and peered around the large chamber. I had no idea who or what I was looking for.

I see him. The little ginger pointed her whiskers in the direction of a slender young man who was feeding birdseed to two caged sparrows. Except these birds were the size of hang-gliders. Several cats cowered in the cage with them, dodging the humongous pecking beaks.

"That's the steward?" I asked. I don't know what I'd expected. Someone ghoulish maybe? Definitely someone older. Not an exotic looking boy of about twenty with dark brown hair, slanted eyebrows and somewhat pointed ears.

Go rescue him, Her Majesty ordered.

"Me?" I was along to open doors. I was no one-woman SWAT team. Besides, he was the cats' steward, not mine.

Go. I saw her claws spring out. The huddle of furry bodies moved off my feet, clearing a path.

"All right, all right." I glanced at the vet again. His back was to me. I could see his tail wagging. I slid forward, silently cursing the so-called Divine Feline for her very mundane, catlike refusal to go near the veterinarian.

The vet turned his bulldog face toward me when I was halfway across hell. I waved jauntily. Maybe I was getting the hang of losing my mind. I barely considered it odd when the vet ignored me.

The steward didn't. His head jerked up as I approached, and his pointy ears pricked. "You're—?"

"Here to rescue you," I said.

His slanted eyebrows lifted in surprise. "It's—?"

"All Hallows' Eve," I said. "When the world of the living and the dead come close together." I thought Her Majesty would be proud of me. At least I'd been listening.

The steward immediately opened the birdcage and the trapped cats streaked out. Then he strode to the wall of crates and began throwing doors open.

This the vet noticed. "Now wait just a minute, young man," he woofed.

"It's all right," the steward said. "There're a few of these animals who don't belong here. That's all."

I noticed the vet had the business end of the thermometer pointed at the behind of a bushy white feline.

"That one especially." The steward grabbed the white cat from the vet's clutches and headed for the hallway. By now two other cats were clinging to his neck like a living fur stole. I and my moving carpet of felines hastened to follow.

"Peter!" the vet bellowed, starting after us. "Come back here. We had an agreement. I do the tormenting, you take care of the demons and feed the damned."

Not that they ever feed us much, one of the steward's neckpieces said.

Cheap brands, Godawful taste, the other commented.

"Sorry, guys," the steward said breathlessly. "Everything was rationed, and I wasn't in charge of ordering." He turned toward me. "Thank God you came. I couldn't have taken much more."

We were halfway down the tunnel, a river of cats flowing at our feet. I felt like a hero in an old-fashioned western. Insanity was way more exciting than my day jobs.

Peter pushed open the slimy door and froze. A three-headed dog blocked the stairway. Behind us the vet had puffed to a halt.

My heroic illusion vanished as I spotted the animal's three mouthfuls of dagger-sharp teeth.

Where do … You think … You're going? it snarled, each head taking two words.

"Out," Peter squeaked.

I thought he could have come up with a better line, but maybe he was distracted by the dog slobber festooning his shoes. He minced fastidiously backward, the cats streaking around him. One moment later I had a cowering herd of talkative cats and one not-quite-human steward behind me and a multi-headed dog growling in three part harmony in front. From somewhere farther in the rear, I heard the vet say something about dewormer capsules and chuckle hollowly.

"May … maybe you better go without me," Peter quavered. "I … I've been harried so much this past year, I can't face the Lord of the Underworld." He stepped toward me and draped one of the cats carefully around my neck. "Besides, you've found yourself another steward." He bowed his head at me.

Don't be ridiculous, Her Majesty snapped. *We need all the stewards we can get.*

Besides, she's a little bird-brained, the Persian pointed out.

I removed the cat from my neck and set it down with the others. I hadn't signed on to be some sort of cat guardian. Or mauled by an under-worldly dog. For that matter, I hadn't signed on at all. I almost turned around to give Her Majesty a piece of my mind, but decided not to. I didn't dare turn my back on that trio of slavering jaws.

"Niiice puppy," I said unsteadily. "I mean puppies."

The three-dog nightmare made a lunge for a cat behind me. I jumped back, moving the whole menagerie with me. We retreated backward down the hallway, the devil of cat hell growling and barking, herding us toward the cold examining room at the heart of his realm.

Something inside me snapped. I wasn't going back. Hell was behind me. My own little house with its thrift store furniture was up the staircase, looking more appealing by the moment. I'd be damned if I wound up in kitty hell because of some arrogant royal feline and a slobbering demon-hound. I was going home, with or without my sanity.

I reached into my jacket pocket and pulled out a handful of dog biscuits.

"Nice pooch," I crooned to the nearest head, and offered it a biscuit.

It stopped gnashing its teeth at the cats long enough to look at what I held. *What is that?* one of the heads growled.

"Dog biscuits." My voice had the same squeak I'd heard in Peter's. "Yummy. Try 'em."

I reached in my other pocket and pulled out another handful. I dropped a biscuit on the floor. One large head swooped down to swallow it. Vicious yellow eyes glared up at me. I dropped another biscuit. Then tossed one toward the wall.

The devil-dog jumped and snapped it in mid-flight. I tossed another, edging my way toward the stairs. The cats and steward edged with me.

I dug in my pockets for more biscuits. "Don't let me run out before we make the blackberry bush," I muttered.

I felt the cats squeeze by me and heard the patter of the steward's shoes on the stairs. I backed slowly upward, three dog heads snuffling for biscuits inches from my loafers. I was down to crumbs when I felt a firm hand on my upper arm. I was yanked backwards and the door slammed shut. I heard the snick of the deadbolt and a triple-thunk on the other side of the door. A series of furious howls were muffled by the heavy wood. I felt the rain and wind on my face.

"Are you all right?" It was Peter, leaning his head close to mine. He was still wearing a necklace of cats.

I didn't know yet. Maybe I never would. I did know I was shaking uncontrollably and cold, so cold. "Let's get out of the rain," I said.

We did, all gathering in my living room to come off our adrenaline high and glory in the return of the steward. And to drink hot tea and saucers of cream. I still had no idea what the steward did for the cats. At that moment, I didn't care. If they were happy, I was happy.

It was almost morning when I fell asleep in the recliner, Her Majesty purring on my belly and the Persian beside me.

The opening of my front door woke me. It was Crystal, home for a surprise visit and no doubt to check up on me. She broke into an odd smile when she saw me.

"What?" I asked, still trying to untangle my way from sleep.

"Where did you get the other one?" She nodded toward the Persian, and I realized I was absentmindedly stroking his gray fur.

"A friend of Divine's," I said.

"Who?"

"Divine Feline, of course." I patted the rump of the little Siamese still in my lap.

She objected to the man-handling with a yowl and jumped down.

"Oh, Mom," Crystal gushed. "I knew you'd like her. She's such a sweetie. And cats are so restful, aren't they?"

Restful! But I'd worried Crystal enough lately with my empty nest syndrome. No sense worrying her with hell-hounds and doors in blackberry bushes. With a vague smile I evicted the Persian from my lap and got up to make my daughter tea.

"The guy outside?" Crystal asked as she accompanied me to the kitchen.

I glanced out my window and saw Peter with a pair of clippers obliterating the blackberry bramble. A couple of cats were at his feet, but he'd taken off the fur necklace.

"Peter Steward," I told Crystal. "He's helping out."

Crystal seemed content with that. I peered around the portion of the yard I could see through the glass, wondering where all the rest of the cats had gone. Home, probably, or on some other kitty adventure.

"You're not depressed anymore?" Crystal asked as we sank into chairs in the dining room. "It was okay to bring you the cat?"

I sipped at the steaming brew and wondered what I did feel. Exhausted. Still jittery from my brush with the netherworld's various denizens. But in a strange way fulfilled. The Divine Feline, for all her arrogant independence, had needed me. And so had the other cats and Peter. And I needed that. I smiled at my daughter. Maybe my nest wasn't completely vacant after all.

"It was fine to bring the cat home," I said. "Thank you."

I heard an unmistakable urping sound from the living room. Her Majesty sauntered past me.

We have left you a hairball, she said.

Susan Skaggs is a retired librarian who lives in Sequim, Washington with her husband and three dogs. She owns a pet sitting and odd job service.

© Raven 2007

SIAMESE

Raven O'Keefe

AMBROSE

by Joan Worley

Benjamin Townsend was forty-five. He was powerful, he was feared, and he was ruthless. He was a happy man.

He stepped onto the podium and faced the admiring crowd.

Out, said the voice.

Benjamin ignored it. He addressed his glittering audience. "Ladies and Gentlemen, Honored members of the Committee, I am not certain how best to respond to the signal honor you do me in bestowing an unprecedented two Nobel Prizes—"

Go out, the voice said again.

Despite himself, Benjamin was flustered. He searched the audience for a heckler, but the distinguished assembly retained a formal silence. Benjamin began his Nobel acceptance speech again. It was too late. Already he felt his feet less firm on the podium. Then his carefully prepared notes began to dissolve in his hands. He forced himself to continue.

"For an engineer the highest—"

Need go out! Now!

The dream vanished, the heady atmosphere of Stockholm replaced by his solitary bedroom. Benjamin rubbed a bleary eye. At the side of his bed stood a small beagle. The dog stared back at him. The tan mask on its white face gave it the look of an inept bandit.

Mystery solved. His dreaming mind had transformed the mutt's whine into speech. Benjamin groped for his slippers. Once out in the yard, the dog went happily about its business while Benjamin looked down on the red-tiled roofs of Santa Barbara and wondered what had possessed him to bring the animal home.

Sally Allwell, of course. Sally of the coppery curls and the winning smile. Sally, with her sweetly cantilevered breasts. He'd wanted his hands on those breasts from the moment he saw young Dr. Allwell presenting a paper at last year's Conference on Materials Optimization in Engineering.

During the coffee break afterward, the interest of such a well-known entity as Dr. Benjamin Townsend had sent a delightful flush to her lovely face. He'd only chatted amiably, asking for her curriculum vitae, but even then an inchoate desire had nudged at his mind. Fortunately, Sally Allwell's academic qualifications were as fetching as her nubile body. The plan took shape.

He would bring her to Santa Barbara, to his department and his bed.

Despite Benjamin's influence as department chair, it had taken months of maneuvering to push Sally's predecessor into retirement, followed by some downright risky plotting to sour the hiring committee on her more experienced rivals for the vacancy.

The same night he phoned to offer Sally the job, he also phoned Esme, his current graduate student paramour, and told her it was over. While he explained that all good things must end, he considered the future. Zaftig Esme would soon begin to sag, whereas Sally's willowy form would retain structural integrity for many years. Benjamin quieted Esme's sobs by hanging up.

By the time Sally arrived in Santa Barbara, Benjamin had long forgotten Esme. He bullied several doctoral students into schlepping boxes from Sally's U-haul to the apartment he'd found for her. Benjamin himself had driven Sally and her road-traumatized cat to an animal clinic for the cat's check-up.

The dog had been waiting, a stray the vet now offered to Sally. Sally looked sad to turn down the beagle.

"Theodosia would never stand for it," she said, fondling an enormous Persian with the face of a hard-used prizefighter. Then she'd turned to Benjamin. "Do you have a pet?"

He'd lost the battle at that moment. He couldn't tell the woman who was meant to share his life that he hated small warm creatures of any species. Seduction required a delicate sense of balance. To refuse the animal might bring instant discredit, and he meant Sally Allwell to be his.

*   *   *   *

Now here he stood, alone in the pre-dawn fog, watching the beast drain its bladder.

In.

Benjamin looked around. No one. Just a little dog at his feet, its head cocked toward the front door. Of course it hadn't spoken; he'd simply felt its impatience. Benjamin was not good with living things, but this little dog seemed able to let him know its simplest needs. He almost smiled as he took the dog inside and began to dress for the day with special care.

Benjamin hesitated before allowing the beagle into his Porsche, but he saw no choice. He must bring the dog to campus. Sally would be in his office to sign her new-hire forms today, and she'd be impressed by a show of fondness for the creature.

The dog trotted amiably at his heels as he strolled to the elevator in the Engineering Tower. During the ride up, it sat alert by his side.

At the door marked Dr. Benjamin Townsend, Department Chair, Mrs. Cumber dithered, her smile even more timid than usual. She waved a Post-it.

"I'm so sorry Dr. Townsend. I forgot to give you this message yesterday. I know you told me—"

Stupid bitch.

Benjamin stopped when he heard the voice, felt his jaw drop. He hadn't said the words, he knew he hadn't, but they had certainly been on the tip of his tongue. He glanced suspiciously down at the beagle, then at Mrs. Cumber. Her tremulous smile told him she had heard nothing.

"Never mind, Mrs. Cumber." For once Benjamin left a reprimand unspoken. He brushed by the woman and went on to his inner office, closing the door on Mrs. Cumber's relieved murmurs.

He sat brooding. Surely the voice he heard was not that of the dog.

Benjamin leaned toward the animal and snapped his fingers. "Hey you, come here."

The beagle trotted over and slipped its head under Benjamin's hand. Benjamin rubbed distractedly. "Let's get this straight. Can you talk or what?"

The dog looked up at him, panting slightly, eyes brown and vacant.

"Talk to me, damn it."

"Yes, sir."

Benjamin's heart stuttered for an instant. He spun round in his chair. In the doorway stood Chuck Platt, fear on his round face. "Oh," said Benjamin. "It's you."

He'd expected the big clod to come begging for another chance at his doctoral exams. Usually Benjamin took pleasure in expelling failures from his department, like a priest purifying the temple.

His mind, however, was occupied with the odd voice, so he sat quietly while Platt trotted out his excuses. Then he explained calmly to Platt that a child's illness did not constitute sufficient reason for dozing during a six-hour written exam.

"But, sir, if I could just try once more, maybe after Jilly goes into remission again."

The beagle stirred at Benjamin's feet, and Benjamin listened again for the voice.

"Sir?" Platt's big moon face hovered over him hopefully.

The beagle kept silent, though Benjamin thought he could see its mouth open slightly.

"Sir?"

"Oh, hell, I don't care." He waved Platt out the door. "Talk to your committee members about it."

"Thank you, Dr. Townsend. Thank you, sir. You'll never regret this. I promise—"

Benjamin swiveled to glare full-face at the man. Platt bolted. Benjamin swiveled back to the dog. "Now. Talk to me."

The dog panted.

After a long minute of rhythmical dog breath, Benjamin pushed the animal away. Of course it couldn't talk. He'd simply grown unused to constant company—even that of a dumb brute. Then, too, he was a bit nervy because Sally was finally here, in his city, on his campus, in his life.

Benjamin considered his position. He had nearly everything he felt he deserved. An acknowledged authority in both structure and materials, he chaired—hell, practically owned—a prestigious Engineering Department. If he could continue to undermine that fool Mansoni, he'd soon displace the old man as Dean of the School of Engineering. In his current position, Benjamin rarely had to teach. He concentrated on lucrative consulting jobs. Such corporate moonlighting had elevated him from off-the-rack Armani to hand-tailored suits; from Saturn coupes to his Porsche 924/931; and from a two-bedroom in modest Goleta to a ranchito in the Santa Barbara hills just a stone's throw from Montecito, where celebrities lay thick on the ground. In due time, Benjamin would move there, too. He imagined lazy Sunday breakfasts at the San Ysidro Drug Store, wowing the film stars with his technical expertise: Man of Science, Man of Steel.

And now, here was Sally—intelligent, young, voluptuous Sally—the final accessory to his brilliant life. Benjamin glanced at the clock. She'd be there at one. He licked his lips. With luck, he'd have her before the autumn midterms.

As he waited, however, Benjamin found it difficult to maintain his usual focus on his own desires. He fell into distraction, listening anxiously for any utterance that might be traced to the beagle. Preoccupied, he did not think of firing Mrs. Cumber for botching yet another letter, though having lasted a month in his employ she was overdue for dismissal. Nor did he shout abuse when the review committee met to discuss an assistant professor's tenure packet. He merely jotted notes for a scathing memo to the dean (cc Vice President for Academic Affairs).

One o'clock came at last. Sally appeared delighted to find the dog in Benjamin's office. She knelt to make an absurd fuss over it. The animal played about her, all its solemnity swept away by her charms. Benjamin knew how it felt. He grew somewhat giddy himself just to be near her.

Sally pulled a lock of coppery hair out of the beast's mouth and looked around.

"Where's his water bowl?"

"His what?" Benjamin had a sinking pop-quiz feeling he hadn't experienced in thirty years. "Oh, ah. I must have left it in the men's room when I went to refill it." He tried for a boyish grin. "I've been so swamped today."

She returned his smile, and he ducked through the door to the outer office.

"Get me a bowl of water," he told Mrs. Cumber.

"A bowl of—?"

"Yes!" he hissed. "You know what a bowl is. You know what water is. Now!"

When the secretary returned, Benjamin was bent over Sally's shoulder watching her fill out her tax form and her LaCoste knit shirt. Benjamin scooped the Tupperware bowl from Mrs. Cumber's hands and flourished it before the dog. He watched it drink noisily. It seemed thirsty. He wondered if it were hungry, too. It hadn't eaten since he'd picked it up at the vet's yesterday. Maybe he'd get something for it later.

Benjamin forgot about the dog and stood contentedly inhaling the just-shampooed aroma of Sally's hair while she finished the tax paperwork and began the Division of Duties form.

"This is complicated," she said. "What percent do I assign for administration, for God's sake?"

Benjamin leapt at his chance. "These DOD's are messy. Nonsense really, but it's best to get the percentages right, or it can bite you at tenure time. I'll be glad to help you."

"Thanks."

Need to pee.

Benjamin stared at Sally. She showed no sign of having heard. Benjamin decided he'd ignore it, too.

"Why don't you meet me for dinner," he said. "We'll work it out then."

Pee. Need to pee.

Benjamin stopped his ears to everything but Sally.

"Dinner?" Sally seemed doubtful.

"I'm afraid it's the only time I have today."

Her brow cleared. "Of course. I appreciate it."

Pee. Pee. Pee. Now.

God damn it, couldn't she hear that?

"No problem," Benjamin assured her, one eye on the dog's jittery perambulation of the office. When it stopped beside the silk ficus tree, Benjamin leapt up.

"I'd better take this little—guy—out right now. Meet me at The Dutch Oven on Anacapa at six o'clock. OK?"

Uncanny, thought Benjamin a few minutes later, as he watched the dog relieve itself under the nearest eucalyptus tree. He could swear he had heard the animal telling him it needed to go out. There must be a rational explanation, maybe his subconscious picking up on the brute's anxiety. Maybe he was not so bad at pet ownership after all. Sally would appreciate that kind of sensitivity. Yes. He would get the dog some food on the way home.

He went with uncharacteristic pleasure into his review committee meeting with George Dimson. Usually the department's youngest Associate Professor rasped on Benjamin's nerves. At thirty-five, Dimson had almost as many publications as Benjamin. In a year or two, Dimson's curriculum vitae might be longer than his own. Worse, some very major players had cited one of Dimson's reports as a seminal article. Benjamin did not like sharing the spotlight, nor did he trust Dimson's protestations that department politics were beyond him.

Benjamin had searched for weapons against the upstart's pretensions, and today he planned to loose his first poison arrow. Dimson's student evaluations for Engineering 101 were slightly below the "Very Good" mark, something Benjamin could use to prick the man's confidence.

The meeting began according to plan. The other committee members saw nothing odd about Dimson's evaluations, but Benjamin waved a copy of the 101 scores, highlighted in pink.

"What the hell do you think we're here for, George, to teach or to gallivant around making a name for ourselves?" Benjamin, who hadn't seen the inside of an undergraduate classroom in ten years, thought he hit just the right tone of friendly razzing. Dimson hadn't expected the attack. As the man began to stammer a response, however, Benjamin felt a tug on his sock.

Play.

The damned dog. Thank God for Dimson's excuses to cover it up. Benjamin shifted his foot.

Play. Gotcha.

The dog had hold of the other sock now. Benjamin shifted again, distracted from George Dimson's embarrassed defense and the reassuring noises from other committee members.

Gotcha. Gotcha. Gotcha.

The hound had managed to untie his shoelaces. Benjamin felt the oozy chill of canine saliva on his ankles. He kicked out fiercely and connected.

"Ouch! What's going on, Ben?" High and mighty Josiah Mansoni, never one of Benjamin's supporters, was rubbing his shin. Benjamin managed some excuse, but as the meeting broke up, Mansoni shot him a sharp glare before walking out with his hand on George Dimson's shoulder.

Benjamin reached under the table and grabbed the dog by the scruff, tempted to throw the beast out the window. He stopped at the thought of Sally's horrified reaction. He took a deep breath. Mansoni would cool off. There would be other opportunities to get a shot at Dimson.

To hell with them all, he thought. Tonight Sally would be waiting for him!

*   *   *   *

The Dutch Oven Café occupied a quaint downtown bungalow across the street from the white stucco walls and green lawns of the Santa Barbara courthouse. Benjamin, dog in tow, arrived early and took a table just inside the white picket fence next to the sidewalk.

"What a darling puppy," cooed the waitress. "Shall I get him a biscuit?"

Meat.

The voice had grown undeniably louder and clearer. Benjamin looked up at the waitress, eager to see what she'd make of a talking dog. She only looked back at him in a friendly way, as though she'd heard nothing.

"Oh, no." Benjamin's voice was a croak. He shuffled his feet miserably.

"I beg your pardon?" said the waitress. "Careful, don't step on your puppy. How about that biscuit?"

Meat.

"A biscuit would be wonderful," Benjamin said with ruthless courtesy.

Want meat.

Benjamin did not bother to reply. He forced himself to confront the ugly fact he'd avoided all day: The dog spoke to him. To him and no one else. Benjamin considered whether he was the victim of a practical joke. Those buffoons in microelectrical systems could have rigged something. He bent and ran his hands over the animal, finding nothing.

He toyed briefly with the notion that he might be suffering some mental aberration but shook it off. Such ailments troubled only the weak-minded. More likely, Benjamin thought with interest, it was precisely because his mind was more powerful that he could hear the animal's primitive attempts to communicate.

This comfortable deduction achieved, he relaxed and focused on Sally Allwell, who was walking toward him with those luminous eyes and that spill of red curls. His gaze moved downward to her breasts, his mind dropping the problem of the dog.

"I hope I'm not late." She smiled briefly at Benjamin and stooped to tickle the dog. "How's your new friend? He's such a lovey-love."

The dog rolled over on its back and let one front paw flop submissively. Sally stroked the white belly fur while Benjamin waited impatiently.

"Would you like a drink?" asked Benjamin finally, standing to hold out her chair. He wanted her to pay attention to him, not the dog.

"Sure." She stood, in her face all the youthful promise Benjamin coveted. "Let me just go wash my hands."

Benjamin sat back down to enjoy the obverse view of Sally's retreating figure. The waitress brought the dog a bone-shaped treat, and Benjamin told her they needed another minute before ordering.

Get meat.

"Shut up you filthy cur," hissed Benjamin.

Not cur. Lovey-love.

"In a pig's eye," said Benjamin, then noticed that a woman at the next table was watching him. He gave her a wry smile and reached down to pat the dog. The dog sank its teeth into his hand ever so slightly.

Meat.

"Will you shut up about—"

"Oh, isn't that sweet. You're talking to him." Sally was back. "I think dogs respond to human conversation, don't you?"

"Somewhat," said Benjamin. He cleared his throat. "Now, what will you have?"

During dinner, Benjamin felt himself riding the smooth swell of a plan well laid. He and Sally chatted about the weather and the beauties of Santa Barbara. After the waitress had brought their food, Benjamin bragged modestly about his own culinary talents. When they began to talk shop, Benjamin smiled at the glow of enthusiasm in Sally's face as she described her work in materials optimization. In a way, he thought, that's what Benjamin Townsend was all about, here—optimizing both his status and his pleasure by the acquisition of this glorious woman.

Tentatively he led the conversation around to her plans for the weekend. He invited her to accompany him to the Light Opera performance on Saturday.

She looked embarrassed.

"What?" he asked.

She would not look up at him. "It's just that I don't think—"

Not mate you.

Horrified, Benjamin shot a look at Sally. For once he thanked God no one else could hear the dog's conversation.

"I'm a new assistant professor in your department." Her blush was adorable. "Unproven as yet." Not for long, if Benjamin had his way. "People might take it the wrong way."

Never mate with you.

"Of course I'm flattered."

Can smell it. She never—

"All right! All right!" snapped Benjamin. He saw the shock on Sally's face. She'd not heard a word of those abominable interruptions. He felt the sweat break out on his forehead. "I mean, you're right. You're right. I just—I just wanted to make sure you felt welcome."

Lie. Want to mount.

Benjamin stomped down Anacapa Street toward his car, the beauties of Santa Barbara now unappreciated, the little beagle scampering to keep from being dragged by its leash.

Slower.

Benjamin paid no attention. Sally's professional scruples worried him. The graduate students he'd seduced over the years had made similar protests, but such token reluctance had yielded to his promise of discretion. Alert as usual to his own self-interest, Benjamin sensed Sally would be harder to convince. Anyway, he didn't want to be discreet with Sally. He wanted to show the world she was his.

Slower.

Benjamin strode on to the corner of State Street.

"Oh, the poor doggie!" A small boy pointed in alarm. Benjamin finally noticed the drag on the line. Now he turned. The beagle sat on the curb, its collar up around its ears, its tongue lolling like a hanged man's. A tiny whine came from its trapped jaws.

"Shit," said Benjamin, and went back to pick up the animal. He started across the intersection, carrying the beast, while the boy ran back to tell his mother what the bad man said to his doggie.

The beagle smiled its dog smile and drooled happily over the arm of Benjamin's cashmere sweater.

Make her mate you.

Benjamin stopped short in the middle of the crosswalk.

"You can what?"

The light changed. Car horns blared around him. Diners on the patio of the State & A Café stared at him. He ignored it all and shook the beagle lightly.

"What did you say?"

Can make her mate you. Walk now.

Benjamin automatically stepped out of the street.

"Oh, sure," he told the dog. "Like you have some magical power of love."

Dog love. Best kind.

"Not from where I'm standing," said Benjamin.

A few days later, Benjamin decided the dog was as good as its word. Better, considering its deplorable syntax.

The next time Sally stopped by Benjamin's office, the dog twined around her feet like a cat, loving her up.

"He likes you," said Benjamin, and forced warmth into his voice to imply "and so do I."

"He's such a dear."

Benjamin patted the dog. "He's my old pal, aren't you?"

"What did you decide to name him?"

"Oh, er, ah. I call him, er—" Mercifully, the phone rang. Sally excused herself and left the office. When he'd finished his call, Benjamin looked at the dog.

"I've got to have a name for you."

Have name.

"All right. So what's your name?"

You not pronounce.

"I'll have to call you something, for Sally's benefit."

Silly.

"I know it's—"

No. Choose silly name.

"You want me to choose a silly name for you?"

What call cat?

"Cat? Oh, her cat. Theodosia." Benjamin nodded at the dog. "I get your drift. She thinks odd pet names are cute." Benjamin pondered. "How about Ambrose?"

Whatever.

"Ambrose it is, then."

Good. Now talk meat.

✳   ✳   ✳   ✳

For some reason, Benjamin couldn't bring himself to think of the dog as Ambrose. Perhaps because it was a silly name, perhaps because he knew it was not the dog's true name. "Ambrose" worked like a charm on Sally, however, whose silvery laugh at hearing the name prefaced her acceptance of their first date.

Not a date, really. Just a walk on the beach with the dog. There followed several more walks, a jaunt into the hills, a swim in the ocean, a trip to the annual dog show. Under the innocent guise of "Let's take Ambrose," Benjamin began to circumvent Sally's professional defenses.

To his irritation, the dog continued to speak. For a few days, Benjamin considered telling someone about it but couldn't bring himself to do so. Even Benjamin's closest friends, if he'd bothered to make any, would have thought him crazy. A psychiatrist was out of the question. Shrinks were merely MD's who couldn't hack the anatomy courses. Benjamin would not give lesser minds the satisfaction of questioning his own mentality.

Benjamin could deal with the animal himself, he decided, though he wished the beast would not choose such odd and public moments to start up a chat. The dog's execrable timing kept Benjamin off-balance. He began to lose the thread of discussion in committee meetings. The most inane comments often went unchallenged by his usually acerbic wit, and twice that jerk Dimson even managed to score off him. Without Benjamin's complete focus on control, the air of tension in the department began to ease, though his own irritation only increased. Students and colleagues alike appeared more comfortable with their once-dreaded chairman, but for Benjamin it was a rising strain.

He considered getting rid of the animal. He'd only taken in the dog to impress Sally, however, and he'd look a fool if he chucked it out now. Above all, the dog remained the perfect bait to lure the woman Benjamin wanted to his side.

Two months into his campaign for Sally Allwell's heart, soul and scrumptious body, Benjamin judged the time was right to make his move. He arranged to take her—and Ambrose, of course—for a moonlight stroll on the cool sands by the harbor. The palm trees swayed with the night breeze, and watching Sally breathe was enough to sweep Benjamin away on a tide of lust.

A perfect night.

As they drifted down the beach by the Hilton, the dog loping along ahead of them, Benjamin made bold to take Sally's hand. She stopped and looked up at him questioningly.

"Sally, I—I love you."

"Oh." She put her other hand to her mouth.

He knew she must be flattered by his desire. He was a nationally known scholar, the chair of a prosperous department, a wealthy man, a powerful man. He was tall, handsome, and stylish. He drove a Porsche, for God's sake. He had it all, and he meant to have her, too. How could she resist his masterful wooing?

"We have more than a meeting of the minds, Sally. We're meant to be together." Benjamin knew she could see his absolute faith in his eyes. He would have her. He brought the whole force of his personality into play.

She took breath in deep draughts but did not speak. She lowered her lashes as though mesmerized, but kept her eyes on his as he leaned close to kiss her.

Then her eyes shot open and she looked down. The beagle had reared up and was giving her leg a brisk humping.

"Bad dog!" Benjamin yelled. He slapped the dog hard across the muzzle, and it cowered in the sand at his feet. Benjamin heard Sally's gasp of horror and faced her, trying to look as pitiful as the beagle.

It was no use, Benjamin realized. Sally had divined his own crude lusts from the dog's behavior, and he'd completed the ruin by striking the beast. He watched helplessly as she ran back down the beach.

An hour later, Benjamin calculated that Sally would have calmed down sufficiently for him to begin shoring up their shaken relationship. He phoned her to apologize, only to realize how complete had been the collapse.

Sally told him that little Ambrose had brought her back to her senses. She'd known that it would never work between them, but she'd been so tempted, until Ambrose … Odd, wasn't it, how foolish occurrences could alter important decisions.

Benjamin agreed that it was damned odd. No amount of talking, he knew, would set things right with Sally. He put down the phone, sat staring for a long minute at the rubber Kong toy she had bought just yesterday "for Ambrose."

"I'll Kong you," he muttered. He sprang up and began to hurry around collecting the dog dish, the dog bed, the kibble, the leash—

What?

"You're going away."

Where?

"Anywhere. Back to the vet's."

No.

"I don't care what you say."

Kill.

Benjamin stopped and turned a stunned face to the animal. "What did you say?"

Kill me. The dog was on its back, legs up.

"For God's sake, I'm not going to kill you."

Vet kill me. All four legs stiffened.

"No. He'll adopt you out. You saw how Sally fawned over you. You'll sucker somebody into a cushy home."

Not.

"Yes you will. You'd look cute enough to somebody who doesn't know what a hellhound you are."

Snarl. Bite.

"You're nuts! If you do that, the vet will put you to sleep."

Your fault.

"How do you see that? You're the one who's planning to make them kill you."

Your fault.

"You're going tomorrow, and that's that." Benjamin hurried from the room. The dog was silent that night, kept itself scarce. Benjamin, however, could not sleep. The dog was a brute, a demon with no real intelligence, but a vicious beastly tenacity. Benjamin did not doubt it would carry out its insane threat. Though he tried to convince himself otherwise, he also had no doubt he'd blame himself if he let the dog snarl its way to euthanasia.

The next morning Benjamin confronted the dog again.

"Why me?"

Can talk you.

Benjamin frowned. "You mean you can't talk to anyone but me?" He'd assumed the animal had singled him out by some vicious predilection.

Can talk whoever. A few hackles had risen at the dog's scruff, as though it were miffed at being underestimated.

"OK then," said Benjamin, relieved. "No vet, no dog pound. I'll find you a nice family. With kids. You can talk to them."

No.

"Really. Kids are always talking to animals. Nobody will notice."

Not like kids.

"No?"

Sticky. Stink.

"You're no spring garden yourself."

Will scare. Snarl, foam.

"Jesus, you want to end up like Old Yeller?"

Your fault.

Benjamin still didn't see that, but he had no doubt the dog could give an Oscar-worthy performance as a rabid animal. Oscar-worthy? Of course! Why hadn't he thought of it before?

"Listen. You've got the whole world ahead of you." The dog regarded him impassively. "You're a talking dog, for Christ's sake. You can be famous."

No.

"No? Just like that? No?"

No.

"You'd be one of a kind. You'd make a mint."

No mint. Want meat.

"I mean, you'd make a lot of money. Have everything you want."

No.

"Why the hell not?"

The dog seemed almost to sigh.

How?

"Well, you'd go on TV, for one thing. Be in the movies."

Be caged. Take orders. Sit. Stay. Roll over. Rescue baby. Take bullet for Eastwood.

"Damn writers, sure. But think of the money."

Not pay.

What was wrong with the beast? It had never seemed stupid before. "They pay you for those things," Benjamin said with exaggerated patience. "They pay lots. For a talking dog, lots and lots."

Not pay.

"Yes they do."

Not pay ME.

Benjamin stopped. The dog was right. They wouldn't pay the dog. They'd pay whoever owned the dog. Trainers got big money. And just think how much the guy who owned a dog that truly could talk ... Benjamin looked at the animal with new interest, but it curled its lips to show glistening fangs.

No.

"OK. No show biz. But surely you could do something with this great talent." He must be desperate, appealing to the better self of the brute.

Not talent.

"Sure it is. You can speak human language."

Not talent.

"No?"

Not dog talent.

Benjamin felt his irritation rise. The brute considered human language a parlor trick. "What?" he asked sarcastically. "Not a great achievement like licking your own balls?"

You try.

Benjamin fell silent for a moment.

"Well, you could explain to people about dogs, what they feel and think." Benjamin thought of the manuals by self-appointed pet gurus. A book by a dog would make millions.

No.

"Why not?"

Not dog work.

"What dog work?"

Tracking, sniffing, rolling in things. Dog work.

"You could help your own species. Train veterinarians." A horrible image of the dog holding degrees equivalent to his own flashed before Benjamin's eyes, but he persevered. "Help them learn to treat dog diseases."

The dog said nothing. Then: *No.*

"Why not?"

Human nose weak. Not do diagnostic sniffing.

"Diagnostic? Is that what you do when you poke—"

Not just courtesy. Smell pain, fear, decay.

Benjamin was out of ideas, and he was beginning to see that the dog would dismiss any alternatives to its current home.

"Why me?" he groaned. "I don't even like you."

You no bargain.

"Then why me?"

The dog seemed almost to shrug its nonexistent shoulders.

Belong with you.

"But why me?" whined Benjamin yet again.

The dog's eyes brightened cynically.

You my species.

"Your species?"

Yes. Son of a bitch.

"Very funny."

Dog joke. Best kind.

No more was said about the pound.

In the days that followed, Benjamin almost convinced himself that he saw a spark of affection in the steady brown eyes behind the bandit's mask. At last he had to admit what he actually saw in those eyes.

It was ownership.

*   *   *   *

Benjamin Townsend was forty-five, ruthless and powerful, when the dog spoke to him. By the time he retired fifteen years later, he was a beloved figure. Few people remembered his days as the university's cruelest tyrant. Dean of Engineering George Dimson recalled old Benjy Townsend as the classic absent-minded professor, always muttering to himself. The dean's wife, Professor Sally Allwell, chuckled at how the irascible Townsend had often been coaxed out of an argument by the soft whine of his ever-present dog.

At the retirement party, everybody made a fuss over the little brown and white beagle. Ambrose was an amazing animal to have lived so long. Professor Townsend had never married, but he and the dog were inseparable. If Fate were kind, said one and all, the professor would have his little dog to keep him company for the rest of his life.

Joan Worley is a freelance writer living in Sequim. For eleven years, she and her husband were privileged to serve the whims of Baby, the Rottweiler.

© Raven 2007

Bubby

Raven O'Keefe

MU MAO AND THE COURT ORACLE

by Elizabeth Ann Scarborough

Introduction: My story was written specifically for a themed short story collection called Cosmic Cats. *The lead cat, Mu Mao the Magnificent, first appeared in my post-apocalyptic novel, set in Tibet,* Last Refuge. *Mu Mao was a wise man, shaman, priest, lama, and so on in all of his former lives until he could have gone to Nirvana but instead chose to become a bodhisattva and return to earth in his highest earthly form, a cat, of course. I was inspired to write this particular story because once, when I went to the shelter, I saw this very sad cat who would not eat and refused to be socialized or even look at anyone. The shelter person said that the cat's master of many years was dying and had sent the cat to the shelter hoping that he could find and be settled into a new home before the person died. Several people had taken him home, but he didn't want another home. He wanted to be with his person and had been denied that. I did not rescue this cat, though I wanted to. I had a houseful already and I knew he would not be happy with us either. I fear that he probably got his wish and joined his master in death, but I also feel that it was his choice. He was not a young cat. He did not want a change. So I gave him a happier ending the only way I really could, with the help of Mu Mao in this story. E. A. S.*

Mu Mao became Aware as he was reborn yet again. That is to say, once more he became embodied, for his rebirth occurred not at the body's physical emergence from the mother's womb, but from the time Mu Mao realized, "Here I am again. Here I go again. What now?" The current body gained Awareness as it was dumped unceremoniously into a cage with three siblings, all as hungry as Mu Mao, reincarnate, suddenly was.

Just once it would be nice if rebirth took place in a lovely home, somewhere warm, with soft blankets laid down for the arrival of the sweet little much-adored and wanted kittens. Instead, Mu Mao the Magnificent found himself in an animal shelter, among many other cats and kittens.

He knew it at once by the smell—it was clean, which was a blessing. And at least there would be some food. Often he was born into the wild, or into some great colony of wild cats. Being a Bodhisattva and helping others work out their destiny and achieve Enlightenment was no easy task when one had to skitter up trees to avoid being eaten by larger predators. Worse was having to avoid being eaten by other larger and more feral cats. Mu Mao was now born into perhaps his thousandth lifetime, the first several hundred of which had been devoted to evolving into the wise person, shaman, healer, priest, lama, hermit, monk, and counselor he had ultimately become, the latter thirty devoted to his reward—being born into the highest possible life form, that of a cat. He found it particularly upsetting when others of his exalted species aimed their teeth at his own helpless little kitten tail. True, even some cats had to evolve, but he found their process unnerving.

Did no one in charge of fate think it necessary for Mu Mao to help his fellow life forms from the standpoint of being a companion animal to some doting two legged being with opposable thumbs?

When he had slaked his hunger and thirst, he researched his current situation by examining closely the papers covering the floor of his erstwhile home. They looked fresh and current and he could still smell the ink so he knew they must be no more than a day old at the most. It was the year of the Cat, according to Asian astrologers, and from the date, within the sign called Leo in Western astrology. The sign of the cat. Very catty. Reeking with cattiness. Very clearly, Mu Mao's current mission would be concerned with events unfolding in the realm of his fellow felines.

"Ahem," his Mother of the Moment said. "What do you think you are doing? Tear up that paper at once! Cats can't read!"

"I beg your pardon, gentle mother," he said politely, "But I can. In several languages actually. Which I also speak, though only after judicious consideration for the sensibilities and circumstances surrounding me. However, other than the information I have already gleaned, the reading matter lining our cage tells me nothing of value concerning our current situation. Perhaps you can enlighten me. Is there some great event in the making within the realm of cat-kind?"

His mother, a calico of undistinguished markings, reached out a hard paw and swatted him across the cage. "Don't get saucy with me, young kit! While you drink my milk you go by my rules. Cats don't read and cats of our clan don't meddle in the affairs of the realm. What business have we with royalty? Did royalty step in and prevent my farmer's land from being sold, the barn which has been the personal domain of generations of my ancestors from being torn down to make a parking lot for a shopping mall? Did it keep my elders from being put down and you and your brothers and sisters and me from being put in here where no doubt we'll be gassed as soon as the kits take the kennel cough? Don't speak to me of matters of the realm!"

"I beg your pardon," he said with what sounded like a small pitiful mew as he washed his face very quickly to try to wash away the pain of the blow. It didn't take much to hurt when you were five and a half inches long from nose to tail tip.

However, a small thing like personal discomfort could not obstruct his duty and so he sought other sources of information. The cage beside theirs was filled with what looked like a vast black and gray striped fur pillow. Mu Mao reached out a paw and touched the pillow. "I beg your pardon, sir or madame as the case may be," he said to the pillow. There was no reply. It might have actually been a pillow—it might have been dead, except that there was some warmth emanating from beneath the fur and the coat twitched ever so slightly as Mu Mao touched it.

"Hey, little fella, don't bother the poor old guy," a man said. Mu Mao turned. The man was looking sadly toward the cage containing the inert animal. Mu Mao, sensing that there was something for him here, rubbed himself against the front bars of the cage and gave a small, cute mew. Manipulative and disgusting perhaps, but effective.

The man undid the latch of Mu Mao's new home and lifted him out, holding him in one hand and stroking his head with a finger. It felt very good. Most nice things that happened to Mu Mao felt very good. Feeling very good when at all possible seemed to be one of the benefits of possessing the qualities of Catness.

"Would that older cat have hurt that little baby kitten?" a woman's voice cooed from somewhere to the left and slightly behind the man.

"I doubt it. But the poor old guy has enough problems without being harassed by a little punk like this guy," the man told her. He wore a nametag. It said "Andy."

"Oh?" the woman asked without much interest, and sneaked a finger around Andy so that she could tickle Mu Mao's chin.

"Yeah, poor old cat is a sad case. He's lived with the same guy for almost twenty years and now his master is dying. The guy thought maybe if the cat came here, he'd have time to find a new home before his master died. But the old cat ain't havin' any. He sits like that with his face to the back of the cage."

"Maybe he needs more attention," the woman said. Her voice carried no reproach that Mu Mao could hear but Andy reopened Mu Mao's cage and returned him to his siblings, then opened the adjoining cage and extracted the other cat.

The other cat lay like a lump in Andy's arms, unresisting, but also indifferent and stiff, a deeply resentful look in his narrowed eyes.

He did not respond to Andy's voice or touch or to the woman's. He just sat there and glowered and pretty soon Andy put him back into his cage.

Mu Mao's heart went out to him, but when he tried to speak to the old cat again, his siblings pounced on him and rolled him around the cage and his mother began to wash him with more energy than was strictly required.

After that, he needed a nap. When he woke up, the people had gone home. The first time he lived in a shelter, he thought that when the people went home, all of the animals would go to sleep. He was wrong. This was when the cats gossiped through the bars and wires of their cages.

"Did you hear?" asked a bobtailed black tom two levels down. "The King of the Cats is dead and nobody knows who the new king is or where he might be."

"That's silly," said a fluffy neutered calico spinster. "How can anyone mislay a king?"

The tom tried to lash his bobbed tail and thumped it against the bars. "It's more a case of the king mislaying his mistresses—and potential heirs. Tom Gamble was a very busy cat. The ladies always liked him and he hated to disappoint them."

"Perish the thought," Mu Mao's mother said, yawning and settling her chin on her paws. "The world never has seen such a lot of scruffy longhaired tawny striped kits as His Majesty sired. And which of them is the crown prince, well, that's anyone's guess."

"His Majesty wasn't much to worry about details," sniffed a gray tabby. "He never did appoint a court oracle."

"You don't appoint one of those," a white almost-a-Persian said loftily. "They are born, not made. Not even by kings."

"Well, whoever was made didn't get recognized anyway. So now here we've got Bast-knows-how-many potential heirs and nobody to sort them out. There'll be fur flying for sure, bloody civil war because of it I tell you." The black bobtail was warming to his subject.

Mu Mao peered carefully down through the screen of his cage. He wondered if black bobtail tom had any idea what a war was like. By now, many generations of cats had come and gone since the end of the world. The warlords had made way for governments which were if no less rapacious at least more peaceable about it. These governments were extremely polite to each other. For now. A cat civil war wouldn't involve nuclear devices, probably, but it could still be an ugly and horrible thing. As the many times great grandsire of almost all of the cats in existence today, Mu Mao mourned any carnage among them.

A frightening thought occurred to him then and he checked his own body. Whew! He had a little sooty black tail and a white chest and paws, black back with a white spot, white belly with a black spot. His face would either be black or have a mask he supposed. It didn't matter. He was not a ginger cat as Tom Gamble and his likely heir were. So the heir was not him. Nor did he feel especially oracular. Therefore, he was free to pursue whatever business seemed to call for him to put a paw in.

As soon as the others settled down for the night, he began.

The first thing to do was get from his cage into the adjoining one, to confront the terribly depressed cat.

This presented only a small difficulty for Mu Mao, who as the most esteemed of lamas had excelled in the Tibetan psychic sports, which naturally included breath, and even molecular control. He simply exhaled all of the air in his body. His mother was not watching. Perhaps if she had been, she would have been alarmed for when he exhaled, he exhaled the air between his very atoms, becoming so small as to be virtually invisible. Thus he could easily slip through to the next cage, after which he inhaled mightily and regained his former kitten size, perhaps even adding an additional ounce or two of air.

Then he padded forward to confront the bitter old cat.

The old one was not sleeping, but brooding with both green eyes slitted resentfully.

"My dear sir, you simply cannot continue like this," Mu Mao told him. "You frighten away those who would save you by your unfriendly demeanor. I have it on good authority that it is nearly impossible for an adult cat to find a home from one of these places as it is."

Mu Mao thought for a moment the old cat would swat him but the poor fellow seemed to lack the energy, and instead sighed, letting much of the air out of himself, though not to the degree that Mu Mao had done.

"Don't speak to me of homes. A home is nothing but an illusion based on the whim of a fickle and callous race. I should know. From the time I was smaller than you, all through kittenhood, I was with him, my true companion, loving him when others rejected him, bringing him mice and birds when he was hungry, licking his wounds. I even submitted to the veterinarian's knife so that my natural urges to mate and sire children would not interfere with my closeness to him. And now, after all these years, he has betrayed me. Dumped me like so much feline garbage, given me into the hands of these people who cage me here, without my pillow or dish, without my weekly treats or my toy, without the drug that gave me the feeling of being wild and free—and without that cruel unworthy man I have loved for so long. He doesn't want me any more. I don't care. I hate him now. I hate all humans and I don't want to live with them. If I must live with another one in order to live, then I prefer to die."

"Oh, you will die if you keep this up," Mu Mao said. "But then you will be with your friend if you do, I suppose."

"What do you mean?"

"You heard Andy. Your friend is dying. That is why he had you sent here to find another home."

"You understand what they say? It means something?"

"You mean you don't? You lived all those years with one man and didn't understand what he said?"

"Well—no. Not really. It didn't matter. I didn't actually need to. He would say things in a kind voice and I knew I could do as I wished and if he sounded stern and pointed at something I knew I shouldn't go back to it until his back was turned. Otherwise, he fed and petted me and babbled to his heart's content and I sat on his lap and purred for him and meowed when I wished him to do something in particular. I must say, he spoke better cat than I did human. But then he stopped speaking to me, would not lift his hand to pet me, and finally turned away from me and allowed others to take me from our bed and put me into a vile case and bring me to this place where you see me now. Perhaps he was bored with me, do you think? I have heard others here speak of how their people became bored with them when they no longer performed kittenish antics such as someone like yourself might do. When that happens, I understand it is not uncommon for the people to simply dispose of one, as has happened to me, and get a newer edition."

"No," Mu Mao said firmly. "That is not what happened at all. Andy explained it to the woman. Your friend was dying. He wanted to see you in a good home before he had to leave, to make sure you would be cared for. Even as he dies, he cares for you and worries for your welfare."

The old cat stared at Mu Mao and a large tear ran down the short fur along the side of his nose. Mu Mao noticed that he had black circular stripes that joined on the bridge of his nose, like spectacles. "He will be all alone and he sent me away to spare me. But I don't want to be spared. I want to be with him. I want to go to him. If I die too, I don't mind. But I can't bear to be locked up in here when he needs me." The old cat stretched briefly then rose to his feet and began pacing in a manner that was extremely tiger-like. "If I thought he would live until morning I would raise such a ruckus that the man—Andy—would unlock my cage to see what was wrong and then I would give him a great scratch and make him release me and I would run out the door very fast and home again."

"Oh, good! You could find it again?" Mu Mao asked hopefully, for he was sure now he knew what his first mission in this young life must be.

"Well, it must be around here somewhere!" the old one snapped. "I know I would find it only—only, now that you tell me what is happening, I have a feeling."

"A feeling?"

"Yes, I think—I think he is still here but I don't think he will be here tomorrow. I think he needs me now. Of course, it is all his own doing that I am here but you and I both know this isn't working. I need out." The "now" and the "out" were drawn out and agonized, and meant the same thing in cat as they did in English.

"Calm yourself," Mu Mao said. "I am here to help you. First, we must release you from your cage."

"Yes, but how?"

"Patience," Mu Mao said. He thought about it. He could make himself small again and slip through the front of the cage, but that would not release the old cat. If he were full grown, and the cage on the lowest level, he could easily undo the latch with his teeth and paws and the cunning of thirty remembered feline lifetimes and prior lives as a holy man. But this was not the case. "Hmmm," he said to himself and then, "Hm?" That was it. A simple mantra, a chant—a purr, done with great concentration and deep vibration.

He leaned against the lock and purred with all his might and all his energy and all of the depth of his tiny being. The lock never stood a chance. It shuddered open within moments, and Mu Mao and the old cat leaped to the floor.

Instantly all of the other cats were awake and scratching at their cages. Mu Mao's new mother was particularly vociferous. "Ungrateful spawn of a lecherous tomcat, why are you liberating that washed up old alley cat and not your own family?"

"Mother—friends, at least here you will have a warm place to sleep and food. Outside you will have nothing."

"Except our freedom," said the bobtail black. "And a certainty that nobody will pluck us helpless from our cages to take us to a gas chamber. I've heard about what they do in these places. Where do you think I was before I came here if not out there?"

The old cat was pawing and mewing at the door and Mu Mao turned from him to the others and back again while the old fellow went frantic trying to get out.

"Very well. There's no time to argue." He went to the door and jumped up on the handle and said to all of the other cats. "Repeat after me:" and began the purring Mantra of Liberation once more.

Moments later two dozen cats and kittens were straggling at various speeds behind the tail of Mu Mao, who was struggling to keep up with the old cat, his face never getting further forward on the old one's body than the butterfly spirals of black stripes in the gray of his sides.

Mu Mao's mother continually lost ground as she shifted kittens and at last Mu Mao in his tiny voice told three of the other adult cats that if they wished to go in the same direction he was, they should help carry the young. Much to his surprise, they agreed. But even more surprising, the old cat turned for the only time since their escape, and scooped up Mu Mao by the nape of the neck. After that, their caravan went much more quickly.

The old cat was not lost, nor was he confused. He unerringly homed in on his former home. A strong chill wind blew them along, but it was not yet raining or snowing and the night was clear, with many stars Mu Mao could not properly appreciate from his berth under the chin of the old cat.

The cortege of cats passed over and under a series of back fences, alleys and yards until they came to a small house with high grass. A light was on in a back window. The old cat dropped Mu Mao, hopped up to the sill and scratched, mewing.

Mu Mao jumped up beside him. The others started to do the same but the old cat hissed warningly at them and then modulated his tone to another plaintive meow.

Inside the room was a bed full of tumbled covers and a small, frail person. The person turned toward the window, as Mu Mao looked on. He seemed to have no attendant or helper, however, and had barely the strength to raise his hand. Someone had brought him water and tidied the place recently, from the look of it. Perhaps he had help come in during the day, or perhaps they slept elsewhere in the house, though it scarcely looked large enough for two people.

"Let me in, Fred! Let me in!" the old cat cried over and over and Fred seemed aware of him but unable to move. Finally the old fellow jumped down, narrowly missing Mu Mao's mother and two of his brothers.

"If he won't open the window, then I will take a run and break through it," the old cat declared.

"Oh, that will be a grand surprise for your friend. A concussed, unconscious if not dead cat lying cut to ribbons and bleeding all over his floor. I believe there is a better way," Mu Mao said. "A moment please." He began his chant of levitation, aiming at the window. It was a tricky business. Once he himself rose into the air and he had to start all over again. Another time he saw something move from the corner of his eye and looked around to see all of the other cats lifting from the ground, and he started over once again. Fred lifted once, briefly too, but then Mu Mao at last chanted with the correct intonation and the window creaked, jerked, and flew open. The old cat flew through it as if he had wings, landing on the bed beside his friend and purring madly, rubbing himself so hard against the fragile body in the bed he threatened to crush it.

"Gently, old one," Mu Mao cautioned. "His fires burn low. You wouldn't want to extinguish them entirely before you had a proper reunion."

Just then, however, Mu Mao heard paws on the sill and turned back to the other cats. "It's a private moment," he told them but bobtail black tom sauntered saucily forward, and had to bounce unceremoniously back to the ground to avoid losing his nose as the window flew shut again.

Mu Mao saw with surprise that the communication between the two did indeed consist only of cat noises on the one side and human murmurings on the other. It seemed to suit them fine, however, and he decided not to offer his services as a translator.

Fred was immediately enlivened by the presence of his feline friend, and gave the cat weak strokes and spoke to him while the cat purred and rubbed. Mu Mao found such extravagant affection almost distasteful, as he himself had learned to practice detachment in all things. However, in his heart he knew that love was not merely a great catalyst to many important changes and events, but the only catalyst if such things were to have Merit.

Slightly bored, nonetheless, Mu Mao looked about him while man and cat reunited. He noticed many framed photographs on the dresser. They were all of Fred and the old cat, who in some of them was a young cat, and Fred a younger man. In one of them the old fellow was a mere fluffball of a kitten and Fred himself barely dry behind the ears. Most of the photos said, "Me and Delf" although one, a portrait of Delf as a kitten, said "Delfy, seventh son of Alison Gray." Delfy himself was very gray in that picture. The dark stripes would have come in later life.

Photographs also covered the walls but they were too high for someone of Mu Mao's diminutive stature to see. Photograph albums were piled on the table beside the bed, as if Fred had been looking at them before his caretaker tidied up. Mu Mao jumped up on the table to see if any of them were open, but none was and they were too heavy for a small kitten to manipulate. He didn't want to knock one off the table and disturb the reunion.

However, from his fresh vantage point, he saw a computer sitting on a table in one corner of the room. This was something even a kit with the right know-how could use. After all, it involved only the pushing of a few buttons and something called a mouse.

It was a small computer, and its power button responded readily to the touch of a tiny paw. Fred was not a secretive man. No password was required to see what concerns he filed on his machine. One choice said "Delfy" and Mu Mao pounced on the mouse. A number of things happened inside the computer with the result that soon there was a chronicle of Delfy's life from the time he was born until Fred became too ill to be Delfy's biographer any longer.

Man and cat had been intertwined throughout their lives to the extent that it was amazing to Mu Mao that Delfy had never learned more of Fred's language or had mistaken Fred's intention when the man sent his cat companion to find a new home. Actually, according to the sad note in Delfy's chronicle, Fred had given Delfy to a friend who promised to find him a home. Apparently the friend had simply dumped the cat at the shelter.

But from the time Delfy was born, a Gemini in the year of the Dragon, when Fred had helped Alison Gray deliver her kittens and had wiped the caul from little Delfy's face, they had been together. There were snapshots of the house Fred and Delfy lived in before and after the earthquake. Fred wrote that before the earthquake, Delfy had leapt from his arms and flown back and forth to the frame of the door, hooking his claws into Fred's pants and insisting that Fred follow him. Fred credited Delfy's instinct for survival with saving his life. There were the women friends that Delfy didn't like who eventually broke Fred's heart and the man friend that Delfy hated, who turned out to be a crook.

Fred even spoke sadly of when he first began to feel ill and Delfy began shredding a magazine that had an article about bladder cancer in it. Had he paid attention at the time Delfy did this, Fred believed the doctors could have treated it.

A Gemini in the Year of the Dragon. Well. Yes. Auspicious? Certainly.

Mu Mao gave the mouse a final, rather unenlightened bat, and jumped down from the table.

Fred's initial joyous greetings had dwindled to incomprehensible murmurings. His pets grew feebler as the joy that had flooded him with adrenaline could not sustain his strength, and his hand faltered, and lay still.

Delfy stopped in mid-purr and looked into Fred's face. His eyes, so fond and happy moments before, were now glazed and empty, though his lips still curled in a slight smile.

Delfy gave a mew that was half a whine and nosed at Fred's limp hand.

Mu Mao jumped up on the bed and with his tiny tongue began grooming the old cat's head. "We were just in time," the kitten with the old soul said. "And you did a good thing for Fred. He was very glad to see you and had missed you very much, as you saw for yourself. I have read his words concerning you and it is true that he only sent you away to save you. But you didn't want to be saved so now what?"

"You who can open doors with your purrs, make yourself invisible and levitate windows ask me what's next?" Delfy asked in a dispirited voice.

"I do," Mu Mao said. "We are all wild again. The others seem to wish to stay together for the time being. How about you?"

The old cat sunk his chin into his paws. He remained snuggled next to Fred's body. Mu Mao licked and licked, projecting calming and healing thoughts as he did so.

"I don't care."

"You cannot stay here, friend. I know the ways of people. Soon they will come and take Fred away and someone new will live here. Probably you will not be welcome and will find yourself back in the place where we were. I think you and I both know you have a life with and a duty to your own kind now."

Delfy turned away to lick Fred's ear, and tried to groom his hair.

A horrible wild yowl sounded from without and Mu Mao jumped upon the window sill in time to watch a gang of strange cats descend upon the refugees from the shelter, tearing into them with ferocity meant to kill. The fur flew, screams and spits, hisses and the sound of ripping flesh met him. For just a moment, the small feline he was in this life thought it best to stay put, but he saw a grizzled calico with one ear leap upon his mother and try to get at one of his litter mates. He levitated the window with such force that the pane rattled in its frame.

The Bobtail black tom flew into the grizzled calico and tore her from Mu Mao's mother's back. Mu Mao was levitating his small siblings to the relative safety of the window sill when Delfy sprang up beside him.

The striped cat's fur bristled until he was enormous, ten times the size of Mu Mao and his brothers and sisters. With a roar like a lion's, a roar so unlike his mewlings and purrings to his former companion that Mu Mao could hardly believe this was the same cat (a true Gemini, he reflected with satisfaction), he stilled the furor of battle. "HEAR ME AND BE WARNED!" he snarled. His eyes were rolled back in his face, and the black spectacles around them became a spiraling infinity knot that hypnotized the cats below and quite surprised and pleased Mu Mao with the definitiveness of its declaration of Delfy's unique status.

"The King is Dead. You anarchists who would rend the kingdom apart for lack of leadership, beware. The new king is among us now. Long live Bobtail Black Tom, the only legitimate and non-neutered heir to His Former Majesty, Tom Gamble!"

The strange cats slunk away from those they were mauling, just far enough to roll onto their backs, as did the other refugee cats one by one, while Bobtail Black Tom strolled among them licking their faces or giving their bellies a warning tap with his paw. Mu Mao's mother, having made her obeisance, brought her youngsters from the sill one by one, the last being Mu Mao, who jumped down unaided.

Beside him, Delfy landed but neither of them showed their bellies to the bobtailed black king. Nonetheless, the king graciously sauntered forward, quite full of himself now, Mu Mao noticed, though he doubted the black cat had had any idea of his own royalty prior to Delfy's announcement. With great ceremony he licked Mu Mao's forehead and then lowered his own head for Delfy to lick his ears, which Delfy did in the feline equivalent of a coronation.

"Great Oracle," the king asked when this was done, "You took your own sweet time about announcing yourself. What kept you?"

Just then Fred's caretaker, who apparently had been asleep in another room in the house and been aroused by the racket, came to the window. "I never saw so many damned cats in my life. Shut up, you lot! There's been a death in this house and—why, Delfy! You came back. Come on back inside, kitty, and we'll find you a good home. Fred wouldn't want you to be a stray."

But Delfy, a true Gemini now joined with his second path, turned his tail to her and nosed the king, who led his court back into the dark back yards and over the back fences and across the shadowed alleys that were his new realm. Mu Mao, his small body weary from his exertions, begged his mother for a ride.

Elizabeth Ann Scarborough is the author of 22 solo novels and 14 more in collaboration with Anne McCaffrey. You can find all of her titles and synopses at www.eascarborough.com. All of them feature animals in one form or another, and most often there is a cat either in the foreground or stalking among the subplots. She currently cohabits with four cats, Treat, Cisco and Pancho (all predominantly black) and Kittibits (a Coony red tabby). Kittibits wants everyone to think he is invisible. All four cats were adopted from the local animal shelter, and have their own outdoor room, a 16x20 cat enclosure on the front of her house. Their hobbies are eating, napping, stealing catnip toys from each other, and thumbing their noses at coyotes through the wire of their cat enclosure (this is no mean trick when you don't have opposable thumbs.) Ms. Scarborough's two latest works, one a novel recently completed in collaboration with Anne McCaffrey (working title Barque Cats—*about cats on space ships) and the other a cat fantasy mystery still in progress, have been inspired by her housemates past and present as well as by Anne McCaffrey's housemates, some of whom she helped deliver (their pure bred Maine Coon mothers were prolific) while writing in Ireland with their human. But they probably don't remember her.*

The Artists

Linda Kemp *developed a passion for handicapped animals after taking care of her eighteen-year-old cat who became paralyzed for his last eleven years. She now cares for the handicapped dog Maggie and cat Hope who gave her the inspiration for the cover art. She lives in Sequim, Washington, with her husband Martin, two other cats, and, of course, Maggie and Hope.*

Torry Bend *is a Los Angeles based Set Designer and Puppet Artist. She is lucky to share her home with two cats and a bin of tireless worms that make productive use of her food waste.*

Phyllis Blakely *is a 72 year old widow living in Sequim, Washington with her dog, Odie, and four cats. She takes part in Peninsula Friends of Animals' TNR program and volunteers for Safe Haven whenever she can.*

Nancy O'Gorman *is a writer, photographer, and web designer in Port Angeles, Washington (www.nancyogorman.com). She has always owned at least one cat, and often several at a time after rescuing them. Her current feline companion since kittenhood is 17-year-old "Champagne."*

Raven O'Keefe *has been an artist since she was old enough to pick up a crayon and ruin her parents' living room walls. These days her primary focus is on portraiture, both animals and people (though she refuses to draw cows). Please visit her websites at www.ravenokeefe.com and www.faithfulfriendsportraits.com. She'd love to do some custom artwork just for you!*

Ali Seeber-Lestage loves animals; that's why she has a lot of pets. Some of her pets are her dog Lola, a Shibainn, her chinchilla Charlie, and her cat Jamie.

Dee Smiley is a senior lady who moved to Sequim ten years ago from Florida. She started painting two years ago, and after being asked to paint a new puppy, many requests followed. Painting portraits of animals and humans has filled her life with friends. It has become a wonderful, unexpected gift!

978-0-595-51810-4
0-595-51810-9

Printed in the United States
122304LV00002B/139-750/P